Endorsement

By Keith Ogden

Pastor, Author and Owner of Timely Bridges Book UK

"As a Musician (1969), Pastor (1974) and Published Author since 2009, I was very pleased when Sarah, Author of "1000 Years As One Day, Life Story of the Choi Family" asked me to endorse her book. This book tells in detail of Sarah and her families experiences, in different locations; times of trials, and much blessings from the Lord. It is inspiring, uplifting and encouraging. I believe the book for Christians will be insightful and challenging. For a non-Christian it speaks of how great our God is, and how real our living and loving Saviour Jesus Christ is. Sarah draws from her lifetime experiences and evangelism and shares them; and how the Lord has led her and the family by His Grace and provision through many trials and situations. I would encourage anyone to read this book and certainly, well worth purchasing, for now and an investment for the future."

"But, Beloved, do not forget this one thing, that with the Lord one day is a thousand years, and a thousand years as one day."

(2 Peter 3:8 NKJV)

About the Author

- Sarah Go-Eun Choi is responsible for distributing tracts, pastoring alcoholics, comforting the broken-hearted, neglected, homeless and wounded people.
- Sarah is the radio presenter for the Choi Family Radio Ministry, broadcasting on-air every Sunday 7-7.30pm at Radio North 846 medium wave (www.radionorth.net) based in Northern Ireland.
- Sarah provides Christian worship music and speaks in local Churches.
- Sarah has studied three years of Doctor of Philosophy in Social Media Marketing, while providing lectures at the University of Ulster.
- Sarah has also written a peer-reviewed Business case study which has been published by SAGE as part of their Business Knowledge series.

Acknowledgements

Thank you to Pastor Keith Ogden for the book endorsement. Also to Dr Paul Robinson who had taken time to write an in-depth introduction of this book.

Especial thanks to all who have made a contribution to cover the cost of printing. Your support has been exceptionally helpful.

I would like to thank all of my friends who had taken their precious time to proof-read this book. Your thoughts and opinions have been greatly valued and helpful comments enabled me to improve this book.

Thanks must also go to our Heavenly Father who made this journey possible. He had given me the inspiration, wisdom and determination to write this book.

Contents

Preface

This book gathers a series of stories which relate to life-threatening challenges, sufferings and hardships which the Choi Family encountered during their Mission journeys in Great Britain and Ireland. The story also records how the Lord has sustained and covered their Ministry with blessings and encouragement. The author believes that the story of the Choi Family mission journeys has its own uniqueness. The story tells of how the Lord had given them the faith, boldness and strength to travel over 150,000 miles and visit 306 Town Centres to share the Gospel in Great Britain and Ireland, being able to comfort the broken-hearted, widowed, disabled and neglected; praying for the sick and caring for the alcoholics and homeless and above all, befriending and directing thousands of people to the Lord Jesus Christ. The author hopes that readers will be challenged and encouraged by the life story of the Choi Family Ministry. Through this book, may the readers long for a closer relationship with Jesus and live for the sake of God's glory.

Sarah Go-Eun Choi

Introduction

By Dr Paul Robinson

After meeting the members of the Choi family as they shared the Gospel message in Scarborough, North Yorkshire, in 2010, I have followed their ministry with great interest. Even today, members of my congregation will tell me of meeting a family of Christians who sing about Jesus and witness to the changes they have seen in their lives and the possible changes He can make in the lives of others. The Choi family take the message seriously, at great cost to themselves, and are faithful in living out their calling as missionaries in a strange land. They serve in the UK at a time when the church seems to have forgotten the Great Commission.

I can only speak of my admiration for their faithfulness and willingness to make a difference to the lives of those Jesus died to save. The Choi family challenges anyone who calls themselves a Christian to relook at what that looks like, and live a life worthy of their Saviour.

1000 Years As One Day, Life Story of the Choi Family, tells the adventures of one family from South Korea as they seek to fulfil the Great Commission of Jesus Christ. Sarah Go-Eun Choi, the author, provides the family background before recalling the various mission journeys of the Choi family. The title of the book is taken from 2 Peter 3:8 and reveals a journey of faith amidst great adversity. In the preface, the author describes the book as a record of mission journeys in Great Britain and Ireland.

Introduction

The author writes that the Choi family journey is unique, and despite this journey not being for everyone, she hopes that her readers may long for a closer relationship with Jesus because of it. Each life's journey is as unique as each believer is. The Choi family journey began four years after the Korean War with the birth of David Chang-Sik Choi, the author's father. In this book, she describes the family situation that the journey comes from. David's father is pictured, although struggling with the political and violence of the Korean Wars, as being involved with the wrong type of people and was led into a life of deception and immortality. This lifestyle created a close bond between David and his mother, but not so with his father. Not only did David endure family breakdown, his home circumstances often left him sick and impoverished. The author describes this as being a time full of hopelessness and sorrow.

1000 Years As One Day

The author places David's world in a non-God environment; his world had lots of gods, i.e. spiritual searching, but no connection with God Himself. One of David's older sisters, attended a church conference and became a Christian. This led her to inviting her family to consider Christianity as a positive alternative to their present existence. Poor education, moving from one job to another and a period of military conscription, played their part in the formation of David's life. A skilled photographer, after leaving the Army, David helped to create a video of a Christian event, and it was there that he met Hannah Myung-Ok Hong, the lady who one day would become his wife. Despite not being a Christian, David had an opportunity to meet up with Hannah, and prayed to the Lord that if Hannah was to be the *'one'* then He was to send him a sign. When he found Hannah, he saw a light shining directly on to her, David took this as a sign and proposed to her.

Introduction

Hannah was from a Christian family and had a much more stable family upbringing than David had enjoyed, as the author writes, *"For Hannah, Church was her second home."* David and Hannah were married in reduced circumstances in the spring of 1983. A major issue was mutual spirituality, Hannah felt that being married to a Christian was paramount; David, on the other hand, was more materialistic and contended himself by smoking and drinking alcohol.

Hannah and David suffered the loss of their first child by miscarriage and their second child died when only four months old. Hannah poured her heart out to the Lord, while David was preparing to send Hannah back to her parents. Hannah was blessed with a third pregnancy, though, and after extra care saw the birth of the author, Sarah Go-Eun Choi in 1987. Her birth, helped to bring David and Hannah closer to the Lord.

1000 Years As One Day

David found it difficult to remain in one place for too long, this regular moving around eventually led him to working as a Sales Executive for a Christian broadcasting studio, where he met with leading Pastors, and was touched by the person and ministry of Senior Pastor Kwak Sun Hee. David felt a deep need to respond to the Lord. It was because of this experience; David felt a call to move to the UK, where he and his family could start a brand-new life with Jesus. On moving to the UK, the Choi family settled into the Korean community of New Malden, Surrey. The author records their time in the UK and their behavioural traits and describes how they coped with life in a new country. As Sarah fought to attend a school where she was not bullied, David studied theology, leaving the family in financial dire straits, leading to taking one set of landlords to court to recover their personal belongings. Despite their circumstances, in the year AD 2,000, David was ordained as a Minister and began to plant Churches in Clapham Junction, Putney, and Kingston-upon-Thames.

Introduction

This was the beginning of their evangelism Ministry, singing Gospel songs in Town Centres, and witnessing to passers-by. Although the Choi family worked hard to meet their own needs, they relied heavily on the Lord, who never once let them down.

Chapter five outlines the results of trusting God, simply entitled *'Miracles.'* The Lord's hand was on Sarah's education, culminating in Sarah's entrance to the University of Central Lancashire in Preston, leading to a move for the whole of the Choi family, which they did with a renewed spiritual vigour. While Sarah attended university, David and Hannah travelled around the North West and midlands of the UK, proclaiming the good news in word and song, David playing a guitar and Hannah a battery-powered keyboard. Whilst David and Hannah enjoyed their mission journeys, Sarah was impacting the lives of her fellow students, leading the international group from a membership of 6 to 170, witnessing 10 students giving their hearts to the Lord.

Chapter 7 details the Choi family buying a caravan and car to further their ministry. This enabled them to witness and minister further afield, a real labour of trust in God's provision and calling.

Chapters 8 to 18 feature the Choi's mission journeys around the UK, Ireland, and beyond. The book is full of stories of adventure and faith, meeting people and challenging them through word and music. This book is written as through the lens of an eye-witness, one is struck by the challenges placed on the Choi family. One constant challenge is to improve themselves as servants of God.

We find in chapter 19, Sarah's decision to study for a PhD in Social Media for Business. Even this is written in terms of a journey with Jesus.

Introduction

Sarah received a scholarship to pursue her studies at the University of Ulster. Along with teaching opportunities, Sarah proved to be a capable pastoral support to the student in her care.

Chapter 20 describes an unforgettable year of new opportunities to share the Gospel message and meet new people who would support the Choi family. Along with the opposition they often had to face, we read of new opportunities of witnessing through the medium of radio.

Chapters 21 and 22 describe the journey from Northern Ireland to London and the beginning of a new mission journey. Sarah writes, *"We feel that we have lived one thousand years and encountered so many experiences, challenges, and opportunities in a single day. As a united family, we will continue to serve the Lord until we see God face to face."*

This book speaks of faith, persecution, miracles, and healing; even in the hardest of days, the Lord has had His hand on the Choi family and promises to continue to do so in the days to come.

CHAPTER 1

Life in South Korea

The Birth of David

After the Korean War in 1953 there was a division between North and South Korea. Many families were torn apart, and divided. Great poverty, suffering sorrow and hurt were experienced by the innocent people who had been affected during the time of the war. Four years after the war my Father, David Chang-Sik Choi was born into a family of six. He was the third child and had two older sisters, two younger sisters and a younger brother.

David's Parents

David's parents met during the war. His father had been originally born and raised in North Korea. He escaped the country during the war, leaving his wife and children, his parents and family. David's father, Mr. Choi, had many tribulations and greatly suffered during these hard times. Mr. Choi worked as a skilled barber, diligently working hard to earn money. As time passed, a friendly old lady approached Mr. Choi and suggested that he should find a wife in South Korea and settle down to create a new family. Therefore, Mr. Choi said, *"If you know anyone, please inform me."*

Marriage of Mr. Choi and Miss Lee

The old lady then approached Miss Lee, *"I know a good looking man, who works in a barber shop. He earns quite a good salary; would you consider marrying this man?"* So Miss Lee accepted this invitation and later they got married. They both then established their own barber shop; and Mr. Choi had another car dealing Business alongside the barber shop in order to make additional income for his family. While dealing with some of the car dealers, Mr. Choi began to mix with the wrong type of people who caused him to sin greatly. His friends were *'adulterers and deceivers.'* They would often cheat, follow after other women beside their own family but in time they became like his friends.

David's Father Leaves Home

David's father would often leave his family and sleep with other women outside the marriage. David's mother would often find out who it was and would instruct their little son David to go and find where his father was. His mother would say, *"Son, go to the street which I tell you and see if your father's car is parked there. Then look up to see if the light is on in the bedroom and wait until the light is turned off. Once it is turned off then come back home."* David knew very little of what was happening, yet, he obeyed his mother and did exactly what she instructed him to do. David would often do this for his mother, even in dark times and dangerous roads, since David cared for his mother and was very close to her. There was one point in time of his life, where his father left his family for six months without returning to his own home and family. During that time, he had found out that his father married another woman and had a child with her.

Despite all this his mother never gave upon her husband. She could not divorce him for what he had done, since she had six children to look after and in those days it was hard for a woman to live without a husband. These circumstances caused a significant amount of sorrow amongst the family members. David grew up in an environment where he experienced a continuous argument between his parents.

David's Home

David's house was built at the top of a storage building and the top floor was built with wood, sand and stones. In the winter, the house would freeze up and during one period of his youth, because of a severe flu virus and stomach disease, David often became sick, and almost died. He was brought up in an extremely poor environment and his father's house was in an area which was not at all pleasant.

As he grew up, David realised that the street he was living in was home to many aggressive and mentally sick people, some of whom were alcoholics, prostitutes, gamblers and deceivers. This place was full of hopelessness and sorrow. During the time he went to school, he would often be involved in fist fighting and his older sister would come and rescue him from this danger. His life was full of unpleasant surprises and this did not help him to live a settled life.

David's Family had No Religion

His parents had no particular *'Religion'* as such. His mother tried various *'gods'* which none ever never really worked out for her. One time, his mother brought in one of the foreign gods. David observed his mother carefully.

Life in South Korea

She repeated a few words and made a wish to this *'god'* by rubbing her hands together, facing towards the south, where this god was thought to reside. Yet, no real change happened in the family. Another time she had apparently received this *'evil spirit'* where she danced all day long, and she could hear voices, which instructed her, David's mother would then instruct the children according to what she heard from this *'spirit'* she received. It brought a lot of fear into the family.

She also tried to go to Mass every day and be a catholic but she felt it was too complex and she could not keep up with this religion. One time, David's father picked up a car from the dealer, and found a book called *'The Bible,'* which had been left on the back seat. He did not know what the Bible was but brought it into the home.

First Time at the Church Conference

David's older sister attended a Church conference and became a Christian. She started going to a Church. Later, David's sister insisted David to come with her to this Church conference. At first, this *'Worship'* seemed quite strange and he wondered why the person on the pulpit was so passionate about the things he spoke about. The lady at that conference seemed quite polite and kind and told David the Gospel.

The whole family (except David's father) eventually began to know the *'Church Religion'* but never really accepted Jesus as their personal saviour. Certainly, David's mother and the other brother and sisters went to Church occasionally and the house environment was a little more peaceful in comparison to what it was before. However, a real repentance and change did not happen in the family members.

Life in South Korea

David Not Interested in Religion or Education

David was admitted to the lowest class in the worst school in the area where he lived. It was extremely embarrassing for him. He tried hard to succeed in this school in order to be accepted into a better school. He was not good enough to enter University, nor did he have the funds to go there. He was later admitted to Arts College where he could take up an *'Acting Course'* to either become a TV presenter, Actor or Film Director.

David's Creative Skills

David was very interested in the creative side of education. Although his dream was to be an actor, he could not fulfil this because of lack of skills, especially in memorising scripts. Nevertheless, he did not give up and applied to work alongside a film Director to learn about filming.

David developed a great set of skills which consisted of filming with a camera, photo shoot, advertising and sales.

David's Musical Talent

David also had very much enjoyed learning to play his guitar and learning to sing all the 1960s records. He almost felt he could be a singer and pursuing a successful career in that area. David's father however, did not agree and became angry, *"If I hear this guitar string once more, I will get a hammer and smash it!"* Mr. Choi knew that by playing guitar and singing, his son would not make a good living. David therefore tried to find a suitable career. However, because of his weak profile, education and career experiences, he found himself moving from one job to another to make a living. As a result he was not succeeding in either his education or career.

Life in South Korea

A Call to Join the Korean Army Force

Time passed he received a letter, calling him for a Service in the army and so David left home, education and work to join the Korean army. A soldier came to categorise and select men who had a distinctive facial structure, no scratches or marks on their face, taller than 5ft6 (170cm) and who were able to swim. Men who met these criteria were put to one side not knowing what was to happen.

Half an hour later, a loud buzzing siren echoed in the field and a group of Chief Police Officers appeared. The men who had been selected were to be admitted to the police army force. This type of army force was renowned for hard training and many resigned with terminal illnesses or died during training.

David would never forget the trauma he had to face during the time of being a police army officer, since Chief police officers were cruel and out of control. During training, if the army officers did not do as they were told; often the Chiefs would beat them with guns and tread on their head with their heavy army boots. It was an unhappy and unforgettable experience.

Riots in South Korea

Almost three years passed and a riot broke out. It was extremely serious that buildings were burning down; terrorists were breaking into the police stations, stealing weapons and looters were breaking jewellers' shops and stealing their goods. Many banks went bankrupt during this period of unrest. Senior members of the Army Police Officers were called on site to deal with this issue.

Life in South Korea

David was in charge of the public transport service, investigating passengers and if any suspicion or sign of a weapon was noted, he was in charge of confiscating this; arresting those responsible and putting those in prison for further examination.

This rioting meant that there was a delay in David being able to leave his three year post. Many innocent people were being seriously injured, losing family members, being left with no homes and many were facing starvation. During the time of his work as the Army Police Officer, none of his family visited him. This remained a hurt in David's heart as he always felt alone and that no love was given from his family members.

Professional Photograph taken in 1966 - Mrs Lee and Mr. Choi (middle), Four sisters (left), younger brother (right front) and David Choi (Far Right)

David Choi (The Police Army Officer)

CHAPTER 2

Marriage

David's Relationship

When David resigned from the army post, he worked in a job which consisted of filming events and special tours as well as working as a professional photographer. He was called to visit a head office of a Christian publication distribution organisation - where a major event was taking place. As he walked through the doors, there was a young beautiful lady (Hannah Myung-Ok Hong), who was the secretary of the company's director.

David was attracted to this lady. He continued with his given task, taking pictures of the event and later he produced a video clip of the successful event. While developing the pictures, he identified a photo of the secretary. The photo came out very well and he treasured this photo in his office drawer. Every time he would come into work, he would open his drawer and looked at this picture. Later he visited the head office of the Christian publication distribution organisation, to pass on the copies of video tapes and photo albums. He then approached Hannah and asked her out on a first date. They met regularly after that and developed their relationship.

Marriage

First time David prayed

David never had much faith in Jesus and yet he said a little prayer before proposing to Hannah. David said to *God, "If this lady (Hannah) is the one to be married to, than please show me a sign."* When he visited the head office and walked through the doors of the Christian publication distribution organisation, he could see a light shining upon Hannah! He knew that this was a sign from God and proposed to her.

Hannah's Background

Hannah Myung-Ok Hong was brought up in a lovely Christian home with her three younger brothers. They lived in a low-class countryside environment. Her father Mr. Hong was a Church elder and served the Church diligently. Hannah's great grandfather had also rung the Church bells, had been an elder in the Church and was diligent in serving the Lord.

There were three generations of strong Christianity background had been behind Hannah. Her father taught orphan children by providing professional education free of charge. In the 1960s he received an award of honour from the South Korean President. Mr. Hong was a low-class farmer, looking after herds such as cows, pigs and hens in order to make a living.

Hannah's Parents Marriage

Mr. Hong (Hannah's father), was admitted as Pilot Army Officer but he continued to serve the nearby Church diligently. While working hard for the Church, he met his wife Miss Kim, Hannah's mother who loved the Lord Jesus and often used her beautiful voice to praise Him. Hannah's mother loved to sing and she had been involved with various vocal groups and entered into many competitions and received distinction awards.

Marriage

Hannah's great grandmother also had a heart of gold, helping many poor families who were under threat of starvation, providing them with food and clothing. Both of Hannah's parents had been raised and brought up in a loving Christian environment.

Hannah's Education and Church

Hannah did not enjoy her education and as she had health problems she often missed school. However, she loved to sing in Church as well as learning to sing country songs. She entered singing competitions and received first class awards Hannah had a great relationship with her school friends but the majority of her friends were from her Church and she did not associate with non-believers outside the Church. Hannah loved the Lord, and obeyed her parents. Every Sunday Hannah's parents would take all their children to Church.

Morning Prayer meeting at 4.30am, and morning Service at 11am and then the evening Service at 7pm. Hannah was involved in the Sunday school, where she played the piano at the Sunday School Service. Later she joined the choir at the Church, while her younger brothers also took part as choir conductor, worship leader and Sunday school teacher. For Hannah, Church was her second home.

Hannah's Career Path

Later, Mr. Hong established a corner shop by the railway station. Hannah had been a shop keeper from her youth, helping her father to run the Business. However, Hannah did not stay in the countryside for long as she moved to the capital city of Seoul to start a career as a secretary in a Christian organisation. She lived with her aunt and her family who were very kind and caring towards her.

Marriage

The only things which interested Hannah were to work, to be involved in Church activities and being at home with her aunt and family. While working in Seoul, Hannah was also involved in various mission activities, visiting the nursing homes, prisons and hospital singing Gospel hymns and playing the accordion. She did not meet any men in her youth. Hannah was extremely shy and quiet but was very committed to the work of God and was a good example as an employee.

Marriage and Arrangements

When Hannah left home to work in Seoul her mother had been busy arranging a man for her daughter. Hannah was therefore asked to come home occasionally to meet some Christian gentleman, who had been brought up in a Christian home. Hannah's mum called one day and said, *"I have a good friend in Church and she has a son who is looking for a woman of faith.*

Their son wishes to establish a Church here and need a helper (wife to help him to work for the Lord)." Hannah did not approve of the idea of marrying a person who was to become a Church Pastor. She did not feel qualified enough to be a Pastor's wife. Although he proposed to her and the engagement ring was passed onto Hannah's mother, the marriage did not proceed as Hannah decided to decline his proposal. While working as a company director's secretary at the Christian publication distribution organisation, she met a gentleman called David. He seemed kind, genuine and caring person. Hannah just wanted to marry a Christian, who was not overly committed but would attend Church with her every Sunday. Little did she know who she was being committed to, since Hannah knew nothing about David's family members and the way he had been brought up.

Marriage

When David proposed to Hannah, there was a little disagreement between the family members. Certainly, the aunt in Seoul disapproved of David as did Hannah's extended family. Nevertheless, Hannah did not listen to her aunt or the extended family members. She prayed about this circumstance and felt peaceful about making the decision to marry David. Before Hannah made an agreement to marry David, they both promised that, despite any circumstances, they would join a Church and attend Church Service every Sunday.

David and Hannah's Marriage

In the spring of 1983, David and Hannah were married in a Church. However, both of them were brought up in a poor family and only had small sum of money to spend on their wedding. Certainly David's family did not contribute towards the wedding.

1000 Years As One Day

David had to use all his savings and received no support from his extended family. Hannah's parents gathered up all their savings to support their daughter's wedding. However, as they disapproved of David and his family, they were very unhelpful towards the wedding plan and received gift of bad quality from David's family.

Wedding rings and jewelleries were to be selected and organised by David. He was not an expert so he politely asked his mother for help and she bought him a set of necklaces, earrings and rings. When David saw the gift he was pleased and never thought to doubt on his mother. As he handed this over to Hannah's mother, she was very disappointed by the quality of the gift as the jewellery was not real gold and sapphire. David was extremely embarrassed but never blamed his mother.

Marriage

Marriage Circumstances

David's mother did not want her son to live separately with his wife. Therefore, David's parents decided to purchase an apartment for David and his wife. Hannah was doing most of the cooking and cleaning for David and his parents. Mrs. Lee did not approve Hannah, as she looked so fragile and weak. Mrs. Lee often rebuked Hannah as she was cooking a meal, or cleaning the house.

As time went on and David started to find work, he would not settle in one place but moved house very often and this caused many arguments between Hannah and David. Life became extremely hard and toilsome. One Sunday, David and Hannah started arguing once again, she was extremely upset and asked her little brother to come and drive David's car to the Church.

David looked out the window as he saw his car was on the road with Hannah on the seat and her brother driving his car. David did not go to Church.

David was far away from God, and often missed out on Church, going after material things such as possessions, money and authority which brought no unity between wife and husband. Hannah would often see him smoking inside the toilet and going to the pub regularly and having a beer with his friends.

Christian Mission Group - Hannah (middle right)

**Marriage of David and Hannah Choi (middle) - David's
Parents (Left) Hannah's Parents (Right)**

"For Hannah, Church was her second home. However, David did not go to Church."

CHAPTER 3

David and Hannah's Calling

Hannah's Miscarriage

Hannah prayed for a child and later she conceived. However, after three months, the Doctor informed her that the child had died. She had to go through a normal birth procedure and the nurses cleaned her womb and hoped that she would be emotionally stable. She was very distressed and David tried to comfort Hannah. Later, in that same year she had conceived a child again. The child was fine and up until four months the child was alive, but then the Doctor informed her once again that the child had died.

This really left Hannah with unspeakable pain and sorrow in her heart. She cried to the Lord, *"Please give me a child. I will give this child to you. I will sacrifice this child to you. I need a child who can help me overcome this sorrow and hardship, a child who can give me hope and joy."* David was determined that if Hannah became pregnant again, he would send Hannah home to her parents and let her mother help her to nurture this child. Later in that year, Hannah conceived again, and this time she went home to her loving mother. The whole family prayed for the child. They also spent money on regular hospital checks. The new Doctor confirmed that Hannah had a lack of hormones which meant that the child would not grow in her womb after a few months of pregnancy. He told the family that as a matter of urgency she should have a hormone injection every month in order to have this child grow to maturity.

David and Hannah's Calling

In 1987, after being separated from David for almost a year, Hannah gave birth to a girl and named her Sarah Go-Eun Choi (which means be a peacemaker in the world). Sarah was fragile and weak but had a good appetite which helped her to grow little by little. David did not want Hannah to go through this painful experience again. So without his wife's consent he had the vasectomy operation in order to stop having children. This unexpected decision did not please Hannah; however, they were very delighted with their daughter. Sarah was very precious to both David and Hannah.

Daughter - Sarah Go-Eun Choi

David and Hannah dedicated their daughter to the Lord. Their passion for Jesus was maturing and they thanked the Lord for this miracle child. David and Hannah both joined the choir at a local Church, serving the Lord diligently.

1000 Years As One Day

As a result of the way David had been brought up, he found it difficult to settle in one job or one place. He had to move around the country at all times. Despite having their daughter Sarah, he was still prepared to move wherever there seemed to be an opportunity to make a better living. As Sarah grew up to primary school age, he moved location so much that Sarah had to move school about five times. This meant that Sarah could not make long lasting friends and settle down in one school.

Hannah assisted her husband every time he ventured on a new Business. He started up Businesses in various sectors, such as a restaurant, café, bookshop, estate agent, video rentals and stationary shop. These Businesses did not last long; often it was on a trial and error basis. David eventually decided to look for a job, after opening and closing various shops, he finally worked in the Christian Broadcasting studio as a Sales Executive.

David and Hannah's Calling

He had the opportunity to meet Pastors from mega Churches and hear their sermons. One time he had to record the sermon of a Senior Pastor Kwak Sun Hee from the Somang (which translates as *'Hope'* in English) Presbyterian Church. David had a chance to see Pastor Kwak preach for the first time. David was touched by his preaching and felt strongly in his heart that he should move his Church to the Somang Presbyterian Church and continue to serve the Lord there.

Church Move

The decision was made to move Church and this was a tremendous decision for David and Hannah, as it meant that they had to travel further from their home, carrying little Sarah. Nevertheless, David and Hannah joined the Church with Sarah. While they were attending the Church there, a post came up and this was a notice to apply for audition. This post was to join the choir of the Somang Presbyterian Church.

David and Hannah had a passion to sing. So they applied for this post. Despite their lack of education, career experience and social standing either of them felt ashamed to apply for this post. They were accepted and were allocated to their seats. David was positioned as a *'Tenor'* and Hannah belonged to the *'Alto'* group. The Choir group consisted of 150 members.

Somang Presbyterian Church was the one of South Korea's largest Churches and the former South Korean president, Lee Myung Bak also served as an elder of this Church. The Church held six Services every Sunday and David and Hannah were involved with the main Service (11.30am). The choir for this Service was the largest and most active group in comparison to three of other Services. Many who were part of the choir members were well educated with high level of degrees, very wealthy and into a good career, unlike David and Hannah.

David and Hannah's Calling

David and Hannah learnt a significant amount of skills while at the Somang Presbyterian Church and worked diligently whilst young Sarah spent most of her time playing and making friends with people in the Church. David and Hannah later became well-known for their diligence and their working hard for the Lord.

Calling from the Lord

One Sunday morning, Pastor Kwak said in his sermon, *"If you want to live a life, life to the full, surrender to God's will and be a committed follower of Jesus."* This message struck David's heart. He could not stop thinking about this message. It was as if God Himself had revealed this to David. He really felt that this message was from God. David knew that he was not living the way he should, he was not pleasing God at all times. His life consisted of earning money and coming to Church. There was no real purpose in his life.

All of his life up until the age 38 was just full of trouble and toilsome. It was time to change his life and make a turning point in his life. At the time David was called by God, he opened up a Business, and Hannah was in charge of a nursery school. They saved enough money to buy an apartment in Seoul and felt very settled. Sarah was admitted to a Christian school and was continuing her education up until the age of eight.

World Business Trip

David had a chance to undertake a Business trip; this consisted of travelling various countries and making video clips for tourists. This gave him the opportunity to explore different parts of the world. While exploring, he had come across a little island called *'Guam,'* a well-known tourist attractions. David had the opportunity to drive in the evening to explore the place.

David and Hannah's Calling

David felt that this place was not safe for his family to be making a new start there. He then visited the United Kingdom. His heart felt reassured as he visited there twice. David prayed in his heart that if God would open the door to this place, this was where David would start a new life in Jesus with his family. When he arrived home, he had researched various newspapers to find a way to head out of the country. There was a little notice, which was an opening to study one year language course at a college in United Kingdom. He contacted them and they accepted his application form. In the first instance, David travelled to London first to see if he could find accommodation, a suitable place to live and investigate further as to how a visa could be obtained. Later that year, David instructed Hannah to close all the Businesses in South Korea, sell the house and let the Pastors know at the Church and teachers know at the school that our family will be moving to England.

Hannah being Pregnant with Sarah Go-Eun Choi

The World Tour - David (middle left) visiting various countries with a group of people

CHAPTER 4

Moving to England

New Malden

In 1995, our family moved to England. We lived in a three bedroom property in Belmont Avenue, New Malden. This place is known as a *'Korean Town in London.'* Nearly a third of the shop signs in New Malden are in the Korean language. This area in South West London is home to a majority of Korean immigrants and students alike. While David studied at the language course in London, he had taken up various delivery jobs and lodging tenants to earn money. On the other hand, Hannah had worked in local houses as a cleaner and carried out part-time ironing jobs to help David.

When we moved to the UK, we had promised God that we would start a new life in Christ, and yet despite the move to England, we enjoyed doing worldly things, such as spending most of our time watching the television, enjoying a pint of beer, singing worldly songs, laughing and joking with friends. The whole family was actively involved in a Korean Church in London. Serving there as a deacon, being involved in the choir, Wednesday Bible study home group leader and being exceptionally popular in the Church congregation. In fact, we were *'Religious'* and pleased men more than focusing our lives on pleasing God.

Korean Church Pastor Kim's Advice

Due to a lack of experience in England, David asked the Pastor Kim for advice on sending Sarah to a good primary school in the New Malden area.

Moving to England

The Pastor's daughter was at a similar age to Sarah and she had been admitted to Burlington primary school, a school renowned as good school with excellent reputation. However, because of a long waiting list, Sarah was admitted to a school in Raynes Park.

Sarah's Primary School

Raynes Park primary school was surrounded by children from a poor community background. Some children were brought up by a single parent. It was a rough community and some children were very aggressive and disrespectful towards teachers. One day at school, Sarah was taken to one corner by a group of English girls. They taught Sarah long list of rude, dirty swear words, and they suggested that these words may come handy later on in life. It was first time in her life of learning such words. Some of the children also had taught Sarah how to steal other people's goods.

For example, there was a lady in school who came once a week to sell stationery such as pencil, rubbers, pencil sharpeners, pens and colouring pens.

Children often would crowd over her and some would take some of these items without paying the money for the items, and without getting caught by the lady. In the playground, some of the boys needed to purchase a plastic football for 50p. They would often steal those without paying. They were renowned for cheating, lying, fighting and swearing. It was an awful experience for Sarah.

Sarah's School Transfer

One afternoon, the sports lesson was ending and Sarah was making her way to the changing room. A group of boys (with freckles and shaved head), were pinning Sarah to the wall. They punched her head for no reason.

Moving to England

Sarah cried and told her teacher what had happened. The boys who had bullied Sarah were removed from the school for two weeks. It was the time where she had to be transferred to a high school and Sarah certainly did not want to stay in this awful environment. Some of her school friends were heading to Coombe Girls School or Holy Cross (the Catholic School). Sarah asked her friends how this could be done, and these girls could not give a definite answer of how Sarah could be admitted to these better schools. Sarah asked a friend sitting next to her, Natalie. She had mentioned that, anyone who is not allocated to a certain school, they would be naturally moved to Raynes Park high school next door. Sarah's eyes opened and said, *'No Way!'* That was not going to happen.

Without discussing this further with David and Hannah, at the age of ten years old, Sarah had made an appointment with an organisation, which helps young pupils to find an appropriate school.

Sarah asked her parents to go with her to this appointment. She met a kind gentleman who was willing to help her. Sarah explained that there was a significant amount of bullying at this school and wished to transfer to a school in New Malden. The gentleman asked a few questions, and then asked Sarah to choose a school between Coombe Girls and Holy Cross. Sarah had said that a few of her friends were admitted to Coombe Girls School and asked if she could apply for this school. In year seven, Sarah was admitted to the Coombe Girls School. The atmosphere of this school was extremely pleasant and welcoming. Not once was Sarah bullied at this school. Sarah was now settled and had a great relationship with her friends and teachers.

Life in London

While Sarah was at school, David continued his studying in Bible theology, after the language course had been completed.

Moving to England

For David and Hannah, living as a theology student meant that the family suffered from low income. Working in the evenings was not enough to pay the rent, utility bills and tax. It was very difficult to communicate this difficulty and hardship to anyone, including the family members in South Korea.

Homeless

One time, our family rented a small room in a flat owned by a group of Muslims. David and Hannah went to the school to pick up Sarah and were heading home. As our family approached the flat, the Muslim tenants (flat mates) would refuse to open the door. The owner had instructed the Muslim tenants to not open the entrance door, as the Choi Family had not paid for the rent that month. David had explained that the rent would be paid; nevertheless they would not let us even take our belongings.

1000 Years As One Day

This caused a lot of problems for Sarah, as she had school uniform on and had no access to the room to take her belongings. Since Sarah was under the age of 16 the government had to help our family to find a place to stay for that night. We had no money to buy food for that night, and the day light was fading, so we hurried to find the place we had been allocated to stay for that night.

When we approached this place, we could see three sets of beds, a shower and bathroom. There was no kettle or any tea or coffee. As we approached the kitchen, we found every single cupboard door locked with a chain. That evening, we were very hungry, and could not forget this day.

Court Case

Our family was extremely upset by this situation, and Sarah had explained this experience to the government representatives. They provided us with free legal aid, which allowed us to have a solicitor to deal with this case. Later that year, our family had to attend a court in order to face the Muslim owners and battle the case legally. The Lord was on our side, and He fought the case for us. The Muslim owners could not fight against the court's decision and we won the case. This meant that we were allowed to head back into our flat to collect our belongings.

Church Planting and Evangelism

Despite the difficult circumstances, David carried on with his studies and in the year 2000, the Lord led him to become a full-time ordained minister of a Christian Church.

1000 Years As One Day

David and Hannah planted Churches in Clapham Junction, Putney and Kingston-upon Thames, serving the Lord diligently. While planting Churches, our family had met a Zimbabwean lady called Emilia. She had studied at the same Bible College with David. She had been helping us with the Church planting for many years. Emilia introduced our family to the open-air evangelism work. She said, *"Why don't we head to the Town and share the Gospel? Take the guitar and electronic organ and sing hymns. I could talk to people and bring them to our Church, Sarah could help also."* David and Hannah agreed with Emilia. From then onwards, the whole family and Emilia made our way to the Town every Saturday to share the Gospel. At this stage we did not know whether evangelism was something which God was pleased with, but because of a lack of members attending the Church, we had done this *'evangelism' in order to bring* people to the Church.

Moving to England

Visa Applications

While living such a complex lifestyle, we had to attend the Home Office in Croydon yearly and wait four hours in the queue, in order to obtain one year visa status. The application was extremely difficult and we were always nervous when it was time for a visa renewal. This process had to be done regularly until the applicant had lived in the UK for ten years. By then, the applicants could apply for the Indefinite Remain in the UK status. This meant that David had to continue with his study for ten years.

When David had graduated from a diploma, he then had to pursue another college to complete another diploma in a different subject. During that time, as a student he had been also working in the evenings to earn money to feed his family. However, because of a lack of finances, David often struggled to pay for his college fees.

In many circumstances, the head masters of the college had asked the reason for not paying the remainder of his fees. Every time this had happened, David was extremely grieved and cried to the Lord for help. For the majority of students who could not pay the remainder of college fees, they were removed from the college. However, for David, it was a miracle when the college administrator allowed David's name to be included in the graduation list. Further, to receive his diploma certificates, despite not paying the remainder of his fees. The hand of God was upon David and the angel was surrounding him.

Psalm 91:4 says, *"He (God) will cover you with His feathers, and under His wings you will find refuge; His faithfulness will be your shield and rampart." (NIV)*

Moving to England

After ten years of living in the UK. It was time to apply for the permanent residency visa. The application costs were about £1,500. Sarah worked as a part-time sales advisor in Johnson's shoes shop to earn money, while David and Hannah worked as cleaners to get money to cover this cost. After saving money diligently and working hard, we went to Croydon to apply for the Residency visa. We prayed that the person who is dealing with us would have compassion towards our family and make this process easy as possible. After asking several questions and observing David's certificates, in 2005, our family was granted the *'Indefinite Remain'* to live in the UK. We were no longer were requested to visit the immigration centre on a yearly basis. This day was a blessing from heaven. God had performed a miracle in our lives.

At the Theology College Graduation - David receiving his degree

Open-air mission work in Manchester, England

CHAPTER 5

Miracles

Sarah's Education

During her time at the Coombe Girls School, Sarah was asked by a group of her teachers to complete an 'Intelligence Quotient' test. This consisted of questions which are designed to assess the level of human intelligence. The results showed that Sarah had learning and emotional disabilities. She was lacking five years of basic human knowledge, which meant that she was not capable of achieving high level standards in her education. Most of her studies, including Maths, English and Science, were her least favoured subject, as she struggled with them.

In all her subjects, she had been allocated to a foundation level and this was a significant worry for the school teachers. David and Hannah prayed diligently to the Lord and dedicated her life to the Lord. Sarah was not highly capable and lacked five years of natural intelligence; nevertheless, she kept her faith and moved forward in life. Sarah failed her GCSE exam and one of the head teachers, Mr. Cuthbert had said, *"Sarah you will never make it to the University with the exam scores like this."* Despite Mr. Cuthbert's lack of encouragement; Sarah continued to try hard to find a way to achieve success in her education.

Sarah's Prayer

Sarah cried to the Lord, *"Heavenly father, will you help me to be accepted into a University? I know that for with men it is impossible but for God nothing is impossible."*

She held tightly to the Lord and faith. Then a lovely verse of *"What a friend we have in Jesus"* hymn reminded Sarah,

"...WE SHOULD NEVER BE DISCOURAGED; TAKE IT TO THE LORD IN PRAYER. CAN WE FIND A FRIEND SO FAITHFUL WHO WILL ALL OUR SORROWS SHARE? JESUS KNOWS OUR EVERY WEAKNESS; TAKE IT TO THE LORD IN PRAYER."

A prayer had been answered, a friend phoned Sarah and suggested that there is a GNVQ course which is equivalent to GCSE and if this course is passed with an overall grade of a *'Merit'*, then BTEC course can be obtained (which is equivalent to A-Levels). This had meant that by completing these courses, there was an opportunity to apply for the University course.

Sarah pursued these courses and at the end of BETEC course she had obtained the overall mark of *'Distinction, Merit and Merit,'* which is equivalent of A, B and B. This grade was acceptable for applying for the University. Sarah received offers from three Universities and it was time to choose which University she would accept and which ones to decline. When Sarah asked God for direction, He made a way for our family to move away from London to Northern England.

Our family decided to close the Church in London, and when Sarah was admitted to the University of Central Lancashire, in Preston, David and Hannah packed all of their belongings and followed Sarah. The travelling to this place was approximately 192miles (309km) to the North of England. This was a new God-given adventure for the entire family; a new beginning for the Choi Family.

CHAPTER 6

Life in Lancashire

Moving to Preston

In September 2006, the Choi Family Ministry began (full-time). This time our family was determined that we ought to live differently from the way we used to live in London or South Korea. This meant that we had to be focused and dedicated to the Lord. Anything which creates a barrier to serve the Lord, we must remove them in the household or in our lifestyle. In order to *'Take up the cross and follow Jesus,'* we had to take into account Romans 12:2, *"And do not be conformed to this world, but be transformed by the renewing of your mind, that you may prove what is that good and acceptable and perfect will of God."* (NKJV) Despite David being a theology student and working as assistant Pastor, planting Churches and attending the outreach programme every Saturday with Emilia, we had always enjoyed watching the movies, TV soaps and comedies. We spent most of our evenings watching the television.

When we reflected on the last eleven years, the way we had lived was not pleasing to the Lord. Due to our worldly behaviours, the consequence was that we had gone through a significant amount of troubles and toilsome life. We were not mature Christians and had been *'Religious'* in many ways. Some of our prayers have been generously answered but on a daily basis, our family was not in unity and often our family would fall into arguments and disagreements.

We could see that God was so loving, kind and faithful towards us in those years which have now passed. Yet, we were not fully committed to follow Him. We all repented of our sins and asked the Lord for His help. We wanted to be dedicated followers of Christ and see manifesting miracles and wonders in our life on a daily basis. Our family prayed for direction and purpose. Psalm 25:4-5 says, *"Show me Your ways, O Lord; teach me Your paths. Lead me in Your truth and teach me, For You are the God of my salvation; On You I wait all the day."* (NKJV)

Change of Lifestyle

The day we moved to no.7 Union Street in Preston, we removed TV from our lives, and have decided to replace all the worldly media by reading the Word of God (the Bible).

On a daily basis, our family had been reading the Bible and one morning the Lord highlighted the following passage of the scripture. It happened to be that Jesus had *"…Travelled about from one Town and village to another, proclaiming the good news of the kingdom of God…"* (Luke 8:1). Then we come across Luke 9:6, *"And they (the Choi Family) departed, and went through the Towns, preaching the Gospel, and healing everywhere."* The Lord was prompting us to visit the Towns in the whole of the UK and Ireland to share the Gospel. The Choi Family opened the road map of the UK, prayed for directions, journeying mercies and then went to the nearest Towns such as St Helen, Northwich, Blackburn, Southport, Keighley, Wigan, Lancaster, Bury, Bolton, Burnley, Leigh and Birkenhead. Due to a significant amount of travelling, the cost of fuel spent each week was approximately £150-£200. It was far too expensive for David and Hannah and they bought a smaller car, which was the KA Ford vehicle to reduce the fuel costs.

Life in Lancashire

Then David and Hannah travelled all around the Midlands part of England to share the Gospel. David and Hannah opened the map daily, praying and asking the Lord for directions. They noticed that some of their journeys each day consisted up to 150miles (241km), reaching souls in the areas of Bradford, Huddersfield and Wakefield. Therefore, David and Hannah decided to part exchange their vehicle with a smaller 1.2 petrol engine size. This would be a wise decision and they could reach a little further distance with a smaller vehicle.

On a daily basis, my father David played the guitar and sang hymns while Hannah played the electronic organ (battery based). The first Midland's Mission Journey was to travel through as many Towns as possible and to fulfil 365 days of open-air evangelism work. From reviewing the calendar, David and Hannah travelled everyday for 730 days (Two years' worth of travelling without a day off).

1000 Years As One Day

It was a magnificent achievement for the Lord. While Sarah was attending the University, David and Hannah started this full-time Ministry serving the Lord and living a real meaningful life for the first time since the day we arrived in the UK. Sarah admired what her parents were doing for Jesus. Therefore, Sarah did not fall into worldly things in the University but kept her eyes focused on Jesus. Sarah had been actively involved with the Christian Union organisation group in the University of Central Lancashire and been part of the music group team to serve the Lord there while studying for the Bachelor's degree. Sarah's passion for Jesus grew stronger and been more mature in Jesus. Later in that year, she was appointed as the *'International Leader'* which was a position given by the committee team at the Christian Union of the University of Central Lancashire. The post was appointed for one year and this role consisted of creating and managing events to invite Internationals.

Life in Lancashire

Providing them with fun and interesting venues with food delights, opportunity to meet and network with University International friends, and most importantly to share about the Love of Christ. This group was initially started with a membership of six people and by the end of that year; the Lord increased the regular attendees to approximately 170 International students. Ten of these students were baptised and decided to follow Christ. During the term time Sarah would join her parents to share the Gospel with the people on the street. Sarah's aunt had given her a *'German wooden recorder'* to play as an instrument, while Hannah played the electronic organ and David played the guitar. These instruments were in harmony and this attracted a significant amount of pedestrians, walking past the street. While her parents had been singing and playing hymns, Sarah also gave out 80-200 Gospel tracts daily, speaking to people stopping by and comforting the broken-hearted, widowed, backsliders and teaching them the Word of God.

As soon as the half-term had been finished, Sarah would return to her studies. During the time our family had been serving the Lord, visiting Towns to share the Gospel, we have seen drug addicts and alcoholics repenting of their sins; backsliders re-committing their lives for Jesus, widows comforted by the Word of God, mentally sick and wounded people were being healed from their diseases.

Evangelism Trip to Stockton on Tees

In June 2007, we drove 116miles (187km), as far as the county of North Yorkshire during a heavy downpour of icy cold rain. We had driven around several times around the City Centre to find a place to park the vehicle, but because of the dangerous weather, it was very difficult to find a place. The wind was so severe that the people passing by would have to tightly hold on to their umbrella, as it would easily turn inside out, trees were falling over, traffic warning was displayed everywhere.

Life in Lancashire

After finding a place to park the vehicle, we were trying to hold on to the car handle, while we were taking our instruments out the car. Then we walked half an hour from the place we parked the vehicle to the Town Centre with the instrumental luggage. By the time we arrived at the Town, we were soaked to the skin, and there was a real difficulty finding a suitable sheltered place to carry out the open-air mission work.

Eventually we came across a white empty shop, but there was a heavy traffic passing by and in normal circumstances, this would not be ideal. We could see that, every foot passengers passing by were forcing themselves to walk forward in order to find a place which was in doors. As our family *'Squeezed'* ourselves to fit in, in this empty shop, Hannah began to play the electronic organ, while Sarah played the *'German wooden recorder'* and David began to play the guitar and sing hymns. We began the evangelism.

1000 Years As One Day

On the opposite side of the road, there was a Bus Stop where people were waiting for the Bus. We could see that people were deliberately missing the Bus to hear our singing. Then some of them crossed the dangerous road to encourage us. It was unbelievable. How could this happen, why would people cross over (in such bad weather) to come and meet us, receiving tracts from us and asking us about the work we are doing for Jesus. We met a guy called Terry and he was brought up as a Christian in his youth but backslid as he became older. After speaking to us and being touched by the Holy Spirit, he repented of his sins and accepted Christ as his personal Saviour. We also had an opportunity to speak to Malcolm, who was drug addict. He wanted to start his life with Jesus. We might not have seen a significant amount of people turning to Christ or praying the sinner's prayer; nevertheless, two souls came to know the Lord Jesus and we certainly have given people the deep insightful impression of what *'Christ follower ought to be.'*

Life in Lancashire

On that day, when we thought that today would be a day of disappointment and that we have wasted our energy, time and a significant amount of fuel costs. Despite the inclement weather, the public generously contributed double the amount of finances to cover the expenses of our Ministry. The Lord did not let us down and was faithful to His promises. We were living by faith, and the Lord knew that we had no income other than the generosity of the public.

Picture taken in Preston (2014)

CHAPTER 7

Purchasing a Caravan and Car

Risky Decision

We opened the map asking the Lord for further guidance. At that time, we felt that the majority of 40 close Towns in Lancashire had been reached, Gospel had been sowed and we had the heart to travel further out to the Southern parts of England. One day, as David examined the newspaper advertisements carefully, he came across a notice to sell a two berth second hand caravan. It is a *'House with a wheel attached to it.'* A caravan had a small cooker, sink, toilet, shower, sofa (which turned into a double bed) and a table. All the necessaries were there to keep us on the move.

The caravan could be towed with a vehicle which had 2.0 petrol engine size. David never drove a large vehicle or towed a caravan; however, this was ideal for our family. Accommodation had always been a problem for us. Even though we travelled a far distance to share the Gospel, we had to return home. The travelling time had been 4-8 hours each day, which was not ideal. We ventured ourselves to purchase a caravan. The owner we met to purchase a caravan was very friendly, kind and helpful.

They guided us with all the necessary procedures to tow a caravan safely and successfully. It was certainly a dangerous and risky decision but for us to accomplish this God given task, we moved forward in faith and risked our lives for Jesus.

Purchasing a Caravan and Car

Once we purchased the caravan, we asked the car dealer to provide us with a suitable car and a tow bar to be fitted at the back of the car in order to safely pull a two berth caravan. The car dealer was an elderly English gentleman with a good knowledge of the car. We had not doubted his choice and he persuaded us to purchase a second hand 1.6 petrol engine size Fiat silver vehicle. Our family had a lack of knowledge about towing a caravan and car. A significant amount of costs went into car accessories. We needed to duplicate a number plate, which was required to place this additional number plate at the back of the caravan. In addition, the tow bar had to be fitted behind our new Fiat vehicle. Car and Caravan with all the necessary fittings, the total costs were approximately £5,500. This was everything we had, given to the work of the Lord. There were no Church or prayer partners to support our needs, no family members we could speak to with regard of this difficulty. All-in-all it was 100% faith in Jesus to move this mission journey forward.

First Day with a Caravan

In 2007 spring time, it was David and Hannah's 24th year of wedding anniversary. David had a strong call and direction from the Lord, to pack all things from no.7 Union Street and depart! This meant that we had to give up our flat, and live in the caravan, touring around to share the Gospel. For some people we were no different to a *'Gypsy'*. We had a significant amount of household items which was brought up from London. It was almost impossible to pack all of these items and to load it into a car and caravan. Nevertheless, because of David's strong demand, Hannah and Sarah managed to fit every single item in the vehicle. By the time we finished loading our belongings, the day was beginning to darken, the temperature dropped and drizzle of rain started to appear. We looked at the map and headed to the South of England. We joined the M6 motorway following the sign to Birmingham.

Purchasing a Caravan and Car

We were approaching towards Chorley area on the motorway, when we could see smoke appearing from the car engine and smell of burning. David pulled up on the side of the motorway. The smoke was extremely severe; we could not open the front car bonnet. While Hannah stayed in the car, David and Sarah walked a quarter of the mile to find the nearest SOS phone box to call for help. The road police officer advised that the vehicle might be in a dangerous state and asked us to stay three big steps back and away from the car. This was sensible advice but it meant that our family had to stay outside in the cold, dark, wet night for 45 minutes on the road.

Eventually, the police arrived and by then we were turning blue, our whole body was shivering. The police examined the situation and he advised us that the caravan and car needed to be moved to the nearest motorway station; which was a mile away from where we stopped the car.

The cost to move the vehicle was £100! It was extremely expensive; nevertheless the police suggested that the vehicle was in a dangerous area and in order to examine the car, the vehicle must be moved to a safer area. It took us up to four hours to sort out this situation. By the time we arrived at the motorway service station, all the shops were closed and the AA service could not be contacted until the following morning at 9am. The first night we towed the caravan, we had no electricity to turn on the light, no power to boil the kettle or heater to sleep comfortably on that cold evening.

We cried to the Lord and repeated the verse Psalm 23:4 *"Though I walk through the valley of the shadow of death, I will fear no evil; For You are with me."* (NKJV) The following morning, the AA Service examined the car and advised us to head back to the car dealer for a water pump replacement. We had no alternative options but to head back to Preston area in order to fix the car.

Purchasing a Caravan and Car

We had assumed that because of loading a significant amount of luggage behind the caravan plus small car petrol engine size would have caused the water pump to explode. As we approached the car dealer in Preston, he refused to exchange to a larger petrol engine size vehicle. He asked us to pay £250 in order to fix the car. We waited 5-6 hours while the engineer fitted a new water pump.

Then we towed the caravan to a friend's house in Northwich. We met Priya in Northwich during evangelism; she was from Sri Lanka married to an English gentleman. She had a young son and lived in a lovely three bedroom property. It was unfortunate for Priya, when her husband left home to be with another woman. She did not want to divorce her husband for the sake of her son. She suffered greatly and often asked our family to pray for this situation.

When we arrived at her house, she had carefully prepared a meal for us. Then she brought in a white envelope with small donations inside with a prayer request. This money was a support towards the Choi Family Ministry. Priya had been a great support for us, as we left all of our household belongings with her and departed on the mission journey. The car was able to pull the caravan easily, since we left our belongings at Priya's house.

We went back on the M6 motorway heading towards Birmingham direction. The first Town we shared the Gospel was Stoke-on-Trent, which were 84miles (135km) away from Preston, then to Stafford, Newcastle, Leek, Buxton, Macclesfield and Tamworth. We were sharing the Gospel in the country of Staffordshire.

CHAPTER 8

Mission Journey in Staffordshire

First Caravan Site

Our first place to park the caravan was a place called *'Stone Village.'* The caravan site was next to a pub where the owners provided a space for our caravan, but there were no electricity connections and we had difficulty with using the bathroom facilities. We had to wait few hours in the morning and evening until the pub would open in order to use their facilities. Nevertheless, because of our lack of experience in finding a suitable caravan site, we were grateful, despite the uncomfortable circumstances.

We detached our caravan from the car and started to travel around the county of Staffordshire.

Charles and Margaret - A Church in Tamworth

We approached a large market Town in Tamworth. During our evangelism, we met a couple who invited us for dinner in the evening. Later that week, we had been introduced to a senior Pastor Charles and his wife Margret at a Church in Tamworth. At this place, they had a large car parking space, where a caravan could be easily parked.

The Church often provides a showering facility for the homeless and they had water and electronic power to connect the caravan. This was an ideal place for us to stay and move around the Staffordshire area.

Mission Journey in Staffordshire

Sarah Returns to Preston

Sarah lived in the caravan for two weeks with her parents, evangelising local Town Centres during her University half-term. As a new semester starts in the University, Sarah had to return to Preston to complete her studies. This time, Sarah had no *'home'* to return to and so she asked her University Christian friends for help. Sarah's friends gave her permission to stay for three nights. However, because of the University accommodation regulation with regard to visitors, she moved to different flats regularly during that term time.

Most of Sarah's time was spent at the library, completing her essays, revising for exams and she had been busy leading International Christian events, attending committee meetings and joining the weekly prayer meetings. When the course was completed and it was half-term at the University, Sarah would pack her suitcase and join her parents for evangelism.

1000 Years As One Day

During that time when Sarah was in the University, completing her first year, David and Hannah visited 20 Town Centres, sharing the Gospel, travelling over 960miles (1,545km), covering the area of Staffordshire.

CHAPTER 9

Mission Journey in South Yorkshire

Lost in Directions

Eighteen days later, Sarah joined her parents. She packed her luggage, departed from Preston and met David and Hannah at the Lichfield Train Station. Sarah's parents already lived in the caravan for 42 consecutive days. It really brought a lot of tears to our family as we all met after being apart for the first time. David and Sarah opened the map and asking the Lord for direction.

We joined the M1 and had been going round and round from one exit to another, five hours had gone past and yet, we had no food or drink since that time. We were running down with energy to keep us going. We bought one large hotdog to have between three of us. We then joined the M1 again! Heading down towards South Yorkshire, we were lost and did not know where we were going with no sign of a caravan site.

Angel in M1

After a while, we could see a car parked at the side of the motorway around 5pm. It was very strange to see a man sitting at the side of the motorway, comfortably reading a newspaper and completing a puzzle! David and Sarah began to walk down towards the vehicle in front of us and knocked on the window. An English gentleman in his 60s had wound down the car window.

Sarah asked him politely, *"Where can we find a caravan site? We have been travelling about five hours and we are totally lost."* The English gentleman said, *"Did you not book the caravan site? I know one nearby here, but let me call my wife and tell her that I will be home a little later than planned."* He was so kind and we could see some hope of finding a caravan site. The gentleman got out of his car and came to ours. He said, *"Just follow me!"* He drove forward and we hurried ourselves to follow him. We arrived at Thybergh Country Park caravan site and the gentleman had gone into the reception to book a night for us. When he arranged a space for us, he came towards our car, shook David's hands and said, *"God Bless You."* We had never met this gentleman and we do not know his name. Nevertheless, we felt that God prepared an *'angel'* for us, to rescue us from this difficulty.

Psalm 34:7 "The angel of the Lord encamps all around those who fear Him, and delivers them." **(NKJV)**

At the Thybergh Country Park, we visited seven close Towns, travelling over 321miles (517km) in the county areas of South Yorkshire.

Jonathan - Dinnington

After five days at the Thrybergh Caravan Park, because of the expenses, we asked the Lord for help. To find a Christian, who could allocate us in a place where it would be a suitable location to evangelise in South Yorkshire area. Then in Workshop we met Pastor Jonathan. He gave us the permission to park our caravan behind the Church car park. This Church was small with a little car parking space at the back. This Church was located in a rough estate where there were often drug dealers and abuse from the neighbourhood. Therefore, the security of the Church was extremely important.

Mission Journey in South Yorkshire

On the day we moved our caravan, we woke up 5am, and without breakfast we made our way to Dinnington. We did not want to be caught up in the heavy traffic. The time we arranged to meet Jonathan was at 9am; nevertheless we arrived at this place two hours early. As we waited patiently, he eventually arrived and we were able to park the caravan. Jonathan gave us a set of keys to the Church, in order to use the kitchen sink and access to toilet facilities.

On the following morning at 6am, we opened the Church gate and the security alarm echoed through the whole Town. We were extremely surprised and called Jonathan for assistance. It was not a suitable time to ring him but we needed to turn the alarm off. He guided us through the security procedures over the phone. We had to secure the place every time we used the toilet. It was extremely uncomfortable and the Church did not have any showering facilities.

Despite this, we were thankful for the Lord's provision. We also felt more compassionate towards people who were homeless or gypsies. We were not in circumstances that were worse than them, nevertheless, we had the experience of not being able to wash and live in uncomfortable circumstances. While we were residing at this place, we headed to eight Towns in the county of South Yorkshire, travelling over 669miles (1,077km). On Sunday morning, Jonathan asked us to share our testimony about the work we were doing in South Yorkshire and lead the worship at the Church meeting. At the end of the Service he would collect the love offering and gave it to us. This was a great help towards covering the fuel costs. On a Tuesday prayer meeting, Jonathan introduced us to two young Bible theology students, Matthew and Brian, who also had passion for Jesus and wanted to gain the experience of sharing the Gospel on the street.

Mission Journey in South Yorkshire

Therefore, we arranged to meet them, at 5am at the Church gate. Then we headed to the city of Lincoln and Grimsby. They witnessed to the people who were standing by and after two days of evangelism experience, they reported positively about the work to the Church in Dinnington. Matthew and Brian witnessed to a group of people standing by and listening to the singing of the hymns (in unfavourable weather), while a particular lady was shedding tears and repenting of her sins. The report was extremely positive and the whole Church congregation had been moved by the positive report from Matthew and Brian.

The Pastor from the Church raised another sum of offering towards the Choi Family Ministry. It was just amazing how the Lord was controlling all the financial needs of this Ministry. On the following Sunday, a few Church members came to our caravan, in order to offer to wash our clothes and to iron them.

We were just so blessed by their loving kindness and the support they gave us during the difficult times of our Ministry journey. May the Lord reward them fully and their generations!

CHAPTER 10

Mission Journey in East Yorkshire

Toll Road

It was time to move our caravan once again. We travelled just over 60miles (97km) to the East of Yorkshire. It was unfortunate as we were driving; we came to the payment junction. A *'Toll road,'* was where a small amount of money has to be paid to use a road. We had to pay £5.40 to use this road heading to Kingston-Upon-Hull. After driving for a whole day, we found a caravan site and this place had beautiful scenery. We were at the East Coast of England.

1000 Years As One Day

The caravan site had a beautiful lake and we could see the birds singing and fifteen wild rabbits jumping and eating grass. We could breathe fresh air in the morning and it was a lovely experience. However, we were not too keen to stay for long, as the owner of the caravan park was not appreciative of our family. We felt quite uncomfortable spiritually and therefore, we looked for a better place where we could stay.

Alan from Skegness

As we headed to the nearest seaside in Skegness, we met a gentleman called Alan. He had been touched by our Ministry, and he offered to buy us lunch. He also asked us if we needed anything else. In reply to his offer, we said, *"We needed a place to recharge our amplifier battery."* Since we were living in a caravan, we had been searching for the electronic power in coffee shops to recharge our amplifier battery.

Alan helped us out and provided us a suitable place to recharge our amplifier battery. The Lord sent *'angels'* like Alan to encourage us and help us out in times of difficulty.

Seaside Mission Journey Experience

On a hot summer day, there were a significant amount of visitors and tourists arriving towards the seaside resorts. For us, it was a great opportunity to witness and share the Gospel of Jesus. We had taken a week to travel all the outskirts of East Yorkshire seaside to share the good news of Jesus. Nevertheless, this type of mission journey was challenging, especially when we were faced with oppositions from Market owners. Often they would call the police and try to remove us or stop us from sharing the Gospel.

Especially in Bridlington, we had an English guy from the Market (selling clothes) asking his younger son (approximately age 9) to go and attack David's neck, to stop him from singing hymns by using a sling to shoot a folded clothes label. What if this was a gun shooting a bullet? It was not as bad as this but being attacked very closely by a tightly folded label was extremely painful for David to bear.

He could not sing for half an hour because of the pain. On another occasion at a different seaside resort, we were singing hymns in a Town Centre. A lady market owner asked us to reduce the volume. She could not bear the hymns being sung. This lady called the police and one officer arrived to investigate the problem. As soon as the officer arrived, an elderly British lady stepped in and said the following to the police officer, *"I had been thoroughly enjoying their singing. You are not here to stop them are you?"*

The police looked at the elderly lady and smiled. Due to this, the police did not approach us or question us.

Barbara and Arthur - Spilsby

On Sunday evening, we were introduced to a couple (Barbara and Arthur), who both worked at a local school in Lincolnshire. They were living at Manor Farm and had a large house in the countryside, and they were also taking care of hens, producing organic eggs, which were given away. As the couple began to understand our Ministry, they offered us a great space for the caravan. This meant that we could travel around Lincolnshire area to share the Gospel without worrying about the cost of covering the expenses of parking a caravan at the site. Barbara and Arthur had been very caring towards our family.

When we met them, we had been living in the caravan for 60 days and had much appreciated their hospitality and giving us permission to use their washing machine and showering facilities. We were so grateful to the Lord for his protections and provisions. As it was time to move on to a different location, Barbara and Arthur left a lovely message indicating that our Ministry was marvellous; *"God Bless you in your work for Him! May the Lord bless you again as you evangelise. Have a good day. With Our Love,* Barbara and Arthur - *Manor Farm"*

While in Lincolnshire, we visited up to 14 Towns and travelled over 1,696miles (2,729km).

Abbey - African Lady's Church Experience

The day we visited a Town called Kings Lynn, Sarah met a lady called Abbey, who was extremly upset and annoyed by this *'Christian Religion.'* As Sarah handed out the Gospel tract, Abbey at first refused to receive it. Sarah looked at her with a smile and said, *"What is the matter?"* Abbey said, *"I don't like Christians, because they are hypocretes and in fact I don't want to know any religion."*

Sarah approached her again and said, *"Please don't walk away but tell me your experience, why you think Christians are hypocretes."* Then Abbey looked at Sarah and wept, as she explained the following incident. Abbey had once gone to Church and the members had told her that the Queen was visiting the Church Service and she was banned from entering the Church premises, because she was *'Black.'*

Then she walked away to find a Catholic Church and walked into the Mass. One of the members at the Catholic Church explained that, during prayer intercession, people had to kneel down. Abbey explained that her knees were not in good condition, she asked if sitting down would be possible. The member of the Catholic Church had removed her from the Church. She cried and walked away and never tried to attend the Church again.

Sarah tried to comfort Abbey from the Word of God. It was extremly hard to convince Abbey that Jesus Loved her and want to know her personnaly. Indeed, the Church incident had been an embarrasing experience, which is quite understandable. This made Abbey reject the Christian faith even more and prevented her from visiting a Church. Abbey needed to fully know the love of Jesus Christ.

Abbey explained that she was visiting the Town Centre to do some shopping and then heard some Church songs echoing. She had been following the noise to see where it was coming from and then Abbey met Sarah. After a long conversation, she had invited Jesus into her heart and decided to follow Him rest of her life.

Max - His Soul was lifted

We were evangelising in North Shield and met a guy called Max who proclaimed to be gay. As he was hearing David and Hannah's singing, Max started to weep and spoke about his life. Max was addicted to smoking and drinking. Max had been stabbed by a knife seven times and had been homeless for 17 months. Max enjoyed listening to hymns so much that he could not move away from where he was sitting.

Instead of walking around to do some begging for money and cigarettes, Max approached people walking past to obtain his cigarettes and continued to listen to the hymns being sung. Max said the following, *"This singing has really lifted my soul today. Thank you."*

Car Breaks Down - Evangelism in Nantwich

As we were preparing ourselves for the next Mission Trip, our Fiat unreliable car broke down once again. Despite this difficulties we had temporarily fixed the car and then headed to Preston to try and fix the car in a more permenant basis. This meant that we had to wait long hours until the car had been fixed. Once it had been fixed, we headed to the Town called Nantwich, County Cheshire, North West England. By then we had been living in the caravan for 76 days and the Gospel tracts were almost distributed.

Mission Journey in East Yorkshire

This meant that Sarah had to find a Christian Evangelist, who can provide a box of Gospel tracts. This was on our heart as we were dilligently serving the Lord. Then we met an elderly gentleman who had been distributing Christian newspapers. He came towards us and said, *"God Bless your Ministry"* and gave us a donation. He said, *"Is there anythingelse you need?"* Not often people we meet on the street ask us this type of question. We knew that this was an 'angel' God sent to help us with our Ministry work. Sarah replied, *"We urgently need Gospel tracts."* This elderly gentleman smiled and said, *"Let me bring a box to you. My house is about 30 minutes drive and it will take me an hour before I can come back to you. Would this be alright?"* Sarah said, *"Yes, we will be here evangelising until you come back to us."* At that time there was a significant amount of rain. Cars had been diverted because of flooding, and yet despite the circumstances he worked hard to reach his home to bring us a box of Gospel tracts.

When he arrived, he explained that, he had been collecting a variety of Gospel tracts over 40 years. He was prepared to give this to someone and yet he did not know any Evangelists to give their tracts to. He was delighted when he met us, since we could be distributing these precious tracts to different types of people in a various parts of England. Our prayer had been answered and the Lord was with us in our journey.

Chapter 11

Mission Journey in North Coast of Wales

Dr Stephen - The Colourful Bow Tie

The first Town we approached was Rhyl. During evangelism we came across a rather strange looking gentleman. He had a mustache and colourful bow tie which stood out from the crowd. He looked rather serious and came towards us and asked a few questions in relation to our Ministry work. Once the conversation finished, he looked behind and there was a cash machine. He said, *"I will be back in just a minute."* He went to that cash machine to withdraw the money.

As he came back, he introduced himself. *"My name is Stephen, and I have been travelling to 11 countries to tell others about Jesus. You are doing a wonderful work for the Lord."* He then gave some donations to Sarah. Stephen gave us his mobile number and said, *"If there is any problems with the police or council, just give me a ring."* He then said, *"Is there anythingelse you need urgently?"* We explained the difficulty of booking a caravan site in advance.

We needed to move the caravan near Wales and requested help. He then said, *"I will contact a few places and let you know later this evening."* Later that evening Stephen called and enquired of a few caravan sites and he explained that the *'Ty Mawr Holiday Park near Colwn Bay'* had a space for the caravan. He suggested that we should move there the following day. Stephen promised to meet us there on arrival in order to speak to the receptionist and complete the booking.

Mission Journey in North Coast of Wales

The following day, we woke up early to move our caravan. It was unfortunate that it had been raining in Wales for so long, which caused the ground to be extremly soft. This meant that our caravan tyres began to sink down into the grass soil. The caravan was stuck and did not move. Our family tried to move it but we could not. Therefore, we waited until we could gather a few more men to push the caravan forward, and this meant that the time we ought to be at Colwn Bay to meet Stephen was delayed by a few hours. As we approached at the *'Ty Mawr Holiday Park'* Stephen came to the entrance and met us. He paid for our stay for few days and then showed us where to park the caravan. This place had fabulous facilities. It had an indoor pool, launderette, restaurant, sports court and convenience store.

It was more than what we expected. We were so greatful for Stephen's help and most importantly, the Lord's provision for our Ministry. During the time we stayed at this beautiful holiday park resort, Stephen visited us regularly and supported us financially until we departed to the North Coast of Wales. His funds helped us to reach five Town Centres and cover the cost of travelling for 384miles (618km).

CHAPTER 12

Mission Journey in Worcestershire and Herefordshire

Searching for a Caravan Site

After visiting the Towns on the north coast of Wales, it was time to move on to a different location. Therefore, we woke up early in the morning to prepare ourselves to move the caravan. We did not mind venturing on to a new location to share the Gospel, but not finding a new caravan site was just a nuisance, since, the site managers would often look at the appearance of a person and judge them accordingly.

1000 Years As One Day

Every time we found a caravan site and visited the reception, the lady or a gentleman looked at us and say that the caravan site is all booked. They have not even considered examining their computer system or their booking notes to tell us that the caravan site is booked! It was extremely frustrating and we could not argue with them about this matter. Every time we journeyed we asked the Lord where He wanted us to go and share the Gospel. Due to this, it was impossible to arrange a caravan site booking in advance. These missionary journeys had to be 100% faith in Jesus. Therefore, the journey was more adventurous, mysterious and risky at times. We were driving over 160miles (257km) from Colwyn to Worcestershire. It was a long time of driving without drinking a sip of water. We urgently wanted to find a place to park the caravan before the sun sets. The Worcestershire and Hertfordshire were flooded and we were finding it extremely difficult to identify a suitable caravan site.

By late afternoon, the day was getting dark, and as we fervently prayed to the Lord, we could see a large restaurant and bar. David and Sarah walked out of the car to seek assistance from a staff member inside the restaurant. The gentleman indicated that there was a caravan site behind the restaurant, but it was flooded and could not take any customers at this moment in time. We were so disappointed with the report the staff member gave us.

A Family Owned Farm Park

The member of the restaurant we visited could not help us to find a caravan site and we were extremely tired and had lost all sense of direction. We needed to sit down, have a meal and rest. The daylight was slowly disappearing and no sign of caravan site. We were feeling hopeless; as we were walking towards our car. Then a smart looking gentleman said, *"Can I help you? Are you lost?"*

1000 Years As One Day

Sarah looked at the gentleman, and responded with a very weak voice to the gentleman, *"Yes we are lost and the daylight is disappearing and we cannot find a caravan site. We are extremely tired and have been driving nonstop since this morning."* The gentleman suddenly said, *"Are you a Christian? I can see a fish on this gentleman's coat."* David nodded and Sarah said, *"Yes we are and in fact we are here to share the Gospel."* Then the gentleman said, *"My name is James Foster and I am a member of the Methodist Church. I own this place. It is unfortunate that you have arrived here when this place is flooded. I cannot take any customer bookings or charge any money in these circumstances. Nevertheless, you are most welcome to stay here (free of charge), until you can find a more suitable place."* We had tears running down our faces when James gave us permission to stay here. While parking the caravan, James came back to us and said the following, *"Our family is joining us for dinner at the restaurant tonight, why don't you join us. Have you had anything to eat?"*

Mission Journey in Worcestershire and Herefordshire

Sarah replied, *"We had nothing to eat since this morning"* and James said, *"You are all very welcome. We can show you our farm after the dinner and we will invite you to our home for a cup of tea."* We were overwhelmed and speechless with his invitation. We had a lovely dinner at the restaurant and had warm fellowship with his family.

When we toured around his farm, he showed us the *'Ice cream factory.'* They produced homemade ice creams and we were invited to try this at their home. Indeed, the ice cream was delicious; we had never tasted such a delight in our entire life. As we returned home and prayed, *"Our Father God, we are thankful for your love, mercy and grace upon our lives."*

Psalm 136:1 "Give thanks to the Lord, for He is good. His love endures forever." *(NKJV)* During the time we were in this place, we visited five Towns to share the Gospel and travelled over 342miles (550km).

CHAPTER 13

Missionary Journey in South East Wales

The Welsh Revival Movement

Our next journey took us to South of Wales. There was a great revival in Wales in the past (1904) and the people who were living there had witnessed the movement of God. Hundreds of people in Wales made a new commitment to Jesus Christ in a single century. This revival was extremly successful and this spread far and wide in a decade in South Korea, India, France and many other countries. The Welsh revival was over 100 years ago and as we were driving, we were surprised to see that the Church buildings were sold to Islamic temples, restaurants, bars and hotels.

Many Welsh people did not attend Churches but rather stayed at home to read the Bible and pray to the Lord Jesus. Our family were extremly distressed by what we were seeing and made every effort to share the Gospel in every Town in North and South of Wales. This missionary journey consisted of visiting nine Towns and travelling over 722miles (1,162km).

Carmarthen Caravan Site

As always, we were driving for five hours from early morning and we could not see any sign posts to indicate where the caravan site was in South Wales. Then Sarah saw a sign post which indicated that the caravan site was half a mile away. David took a sharp turning on the left and drove in a two way narrow road. It was an extremely dangerous road and we came across large vehicles rushing past our car and caravan. Every time cars passed us, the caravan shook. Drivers were not careful about the speed limit.

Missionary Journey in South East Wales

We must have driven over half a mile and could not see the sign for the caravan site. The long narrow road was not ending and we could not see any place to turn around the caravan and head back out to the main road. Then there was a sign to indicate that this road led to the caravan site. Without being cautious, David made a quick fast sharp turning to the left.

The paths we have now joined were extremely deep, and without any concern, we followed the sign to the reception. It was no surprise when the receptionist said the place was fully booked. As we were climbing up the path way to join the busy narrow road, it was impossible to turn right. As the cars were rushing past from both ways, the path way was so deep that the car was positioned upright with the heavy caravan pulling the car backwards and we could smell the car tyre burning.

1000 Years As One Day

Sarah could feel the car moving backwards and panicked, and screamed, *"Dad put the break on!"* David shouted and said, *"I am doing so but the car is rolling backwards, I cannot control this anymore!"* Our faces were turning red, trembling with fear. We reversed the car to the level ground and tried to accelerate the car forward again to the joining point to turn right but the narrow road was extremely busy, that the cars would not give way. In the end, David reversed the car back again and Sarah and Hannah walked in front of the car, stand in the middle of the road and wave until the car would stop either side in order to turn right. It was a risky situation, since there was a great chance that Sarah and Hannah could be run over by a car. On the other hand, if David continued to stay upright and the car breaks gave up then David would have rolled back and caused a serious injury. As Sarah and Hannah prayed, cars stopped on either side giving a signal for David to accelerate forward.

It was extremely hard to come out of this deep end of the path way road. We could never forget the experience we had to go through and how the Lord was with us in those circumstances.

Top of the Hill

The scenery in Wales was spectacular but many areas were extremely dangerous to drive the car and caravan, especially driving on a wet weather on an unfamiliar road. Wales is surrounded by high hillsides and the road was up and down, extremely bumpy and narrow. As we approached the caravan site, the owner accepted cash payment and gave us permission to park the caravan. We should have seen the place where the owner allocated us first before making the payment, but we were desperate to find a place to park the caravan.

It was very clear that the Welsh Caravan site owner did not appreciate our family, as our appearance looked exactly like the *'Chinese Gypsies.'* The owner was not friendly and looked extremely tough. He went in his 4x4 vehicle and said, *"Follow this vehicle!"* Without any doubt, we followed him to the top of the hill. There were many spaces near the reception office but he drove right to the top. Since this was the first time, David was towing a caravan, he found it very difficult driving up the hill, nevertheless he followed the site owner to the top of the hill. David could see on his left car window that we were up on a 300ft hill and could feel the caravan tyre slipping off the edge of the hill as he was driving the caravan to the top. The caravan owner did not provide a socket to connect the electricity and the area we parked the caravan was not a suitable place to sleep in the evening in unfavourable weather such as that day. In the evening the temperature dropped and the 20-30 mph wind was rushing pass the caravan.

We could feel at night the caravan was shaking and we were afraid that the tyres would roll down the hill. It would have been a disastrous death for the Choi Family. Nevertheless, as we prayed throughout the night, the *'angel'* encamped all around us and protected us until the morning.

St. David's - Funeral Service

St. David's Town is the Britain's smallest city in terms of size and population. This was our last Town to visit in Wales. We woke up early to travel to this place and not long after we started to begin our evangelism, an Anglican Minister came and made us stop evangelising. He said, *"There is a funeral Service, inside this Church. You may begin to play music again once the funeral car has departed the Church."* We were singing *'How Great Thou Art'* should this hymn not be played during the funeral Service?

If he was a Christian minister, should he not be encouraging us to share the good news of Jesus? We waited two hours, outside in the cold until we could sing again. Despite the revival which happened over 100 years ago, Welsh people's faith began to be watered down and we could feel the cold air rushing past us as we were sharing the Gospel. We prayed for Wales as we fervently shared the Gospel in these areas.

CHAPTER 14

Missionary Journey in Republic of Ireland

Ferry to the Republic of Ireland

We woke up early in the morning to find a place to share the Gospel, but we were going round and round without finding any suitable pitch to sing. Perhaps the Lord had a different idea. Then we saw a sign which was leading to a ferry port. From St. David's we saw a large ferry carrying fleets of heavy vehicles, including caravans and cars. We asked the receptionist how we could get on the ferry. Apparently this ferry was heading to the Republic of Ireland. We have heard about this place but never visited or have driven around this area before.

It was a risky decision as to how we were supposed to load our caravan on to the ferry and travel around in the Republic of Ireland. We felt that, if this was God's will then He would allow us get on this ferry. By faith, David and Sarah enquired about purchasing a ferry ticket to the Republic of Ireland. It happened to be that ferry we saw which was departing in an hour's time and there were three seats available and a space for the two berth caravan and a car.

The ticketing process was extremely simple and quite unbelievable. The money we had in our hands was the exact money to cover the cost. We knew that this was a sign from God that we should make our way to the place called the Republic of Ireland and preach the Gospel. We were extremely nervous about driving our large vehicle into the ferry. We just followed the driver in front of us.

Missionary Journey in Republic of Ireland

It all seemed fine, and there were people guiding us throughout the journey. It was quite exciting but at the same time extremely nervous and risky. As we arrived on the other side of the Port of Rosslare, we followed the sign to Waterford. We travelled over 154miles (248km). It was very strange to see a combination of English and Irish language written on the same sign posts. Furthermore, the people in Ireland also did not accept pound coins or notes and it was all in Euros. We did not take any Euros with us and this was a little concern for our family. The climate was no different to the place in Wales; it was windy and raining at all times. The place seemed beautiful and peaceful. However, the drivers had a little bit of temper (just like the Koreans) where they cannot face slow drivers. If the Irish saw a vehicle that is driving in a low speed, they would push down the horn 'BEEP! BEEP!' not once but twice to make sure you speed up. It was a terrifying experience, driving fast and trying to find out where we were heading, with our caravan behind us.

1000 Years As One Day

Irish Catholics

As we were travelling, we could not see any Churches. They all seemed to be Catholics, since we could see statues of Mary, the Apostles and Jesus. We urgently needed help with parking the caravan, so we entered the Catholic Church Mass Service and taken part in the Holy Communion, and then asked the Priest for help. Thankfully, the Catholic Priest offered us a place to park the caravan and then we headed to the Town of Waterford to share the Gospel. The responses from the people walking pass, it was quite unbelievably positive. First day and we have seen several people weeping and singing along hymns and clapping. The majority of the people we came across were Irish Catholic members. They were very open to the Gospel, and seek to have a deeper relationship with Jesus. Sarah had the privilege of telling the Catholics, there is more to life than the old habit of *'Religious'* practices. Walk with Jesus, talk with Jesus and tell Jesus directly all your sins and ask for forgiveness.

Missionary Journey in Republic of Ireland

When Jesus was on the Cross, the Temple curtain was torn in two; we now have the great privilege to know God and call Him our Heavenly Father. This personal relationship is what you need my dear Catholic friends. Some Catholics asked where they could obtain the Holy Bible; since they were hungry for the Word of God. The Irish Catholics explained that their Priests would read some passages of the Bible during the Mass times, but they did not have their personal Bible. They wanted to obtain one for themselves and read the Word of God. Sarah indicated where to contact in order to obtain their personal Bible and encouraged them to read the whole Bible on a day-to-day basis. Irish Catholics were so lovely, genuine and kind. We thoroughly enjoyed having fellowship with them and got to know them. Sharing the Gospel in Ireland was not too bad and it was not scary as we predicted.

Thomas - Graveyard

While evangelising in Waterford, one gentleman wept while listening to the hymn *'Nearer my God to Thee.'* This gentleman was called Thomas. He explained about his tragedy of his daughter's death by a car accident. We had the opportunity to comfort Thomas. He wanted us to attend the Catholic Church on Sunday, where he wanted to show us the graveyard of his daughter, which was behind the Catholic Church in Cork. Therefore, on Sunday we agreed to meet Thomas at the Waterford Tower at 6.30am. Thomas allowed us to park our caravan at his home for two days. Therefore, we towed the caravan and parked our caravan at Thomas's place. We travelled 140km (87miles) from Waterford to Cork. We left the car and caravan at Thomas's place and then he took us in his vehicle and travelled to the Catholic Church for Mass Service in Cork. Once the Mass was over, he invited our family for dinner.

Missionary Journey in Republic of Ireland

His house was old fashioned, where he had the stove to heat the water and baked homemade bread. He lived very humbly and was faithful to God. We really appreciated his warm and kind hospitality. We stayed with Thomas for the following two days. While at this place, we shared the Gospel in Kilkenny and Carlow. It was July and yet the weather was appalling. It was cold, wet because of severe down pours and thunderstorms. Despite the weather, we made every effort to share the Gospel in the Southern part of Ireland. Due to the difficulty of finding a suitable caravan site in the area of Wexford, South Ireland, Thomas introduced a friend called Michael. He lived in a rural farming area and had a space which could be ideal for caravan parking.

Michael's Place

We followed Thomas's guidance and drove to Michael's place. As we approached the area, there was a split into two narrow roads; the street on the left was lovely, clean and beautiful and the other street on the right was dirty, messy and full of insects. Sarah looked at the Thomas's instructions. It stated to turn *'Right.'* We were not too pleased but made our way into the pathway to the right. As we approached at the Michael's place, a gentleman who had rough clothes approached us. He said, *"Are you the Evangelists?"* We replied, *"Yes, and are you Thomas's friend Michael?"* and he replied, *"Yes I am he."*

He invited us to his house but because of the condition of the place, we parked our caravan and rushed into the Town to share the Gospel. When we came back, we could see five dogs and one cat.

One of the dogs was a lovely Golden Labrador. However, the only problem with these pets were that they were unclean, unwashed and they were flea ridden. Probably, if they were taken to the vets, the Doctor would have given them some tablets or injections to prevent them from itching.

All five dogs were rotating their bodies to rub their bottom on the ground, and this prevented their bottom to be red and sore. We felt very uncomfortable leaving the caravan and walking into the car. We could not afford to have this itching disease, since we knew no Doctors in this area. Therefore, it was unfortunate that we had to leave Michael's hospitality and move elsewhere to share the Gospel.

1000 Years As One Day

Gypsy's Caravan Site

After driving hours, we turned into a rural area of Ireland. Indeed, finding a caravan site in Ireland was a nightmare! As we approached an area where there were livestock of sheep, cows and horses, we saw some caravans parked in one area. This place looked like a small car park which was used as a *'Caravan Site'* we thought. As we approached at this place, a gentleman crossed his arms as he looked at us moving forward into the caravan parking space. Little did we know that there was a great long barrier just above our car to prevent people from parking their caravans.

We smiled at the furious looking gentleman and said, *"Can we come inside and park our caravan here?"* The gentleman had no reply, so David pushed down the accelerator and then Sarah heard the *'Big crash!'* and said, *"Dad stop the car, I heard something!"*

148

David said, *"It must have been the bumpy ground"* so he stepped on to the accelerator again to move forward. Then Sarah heard the same noise. The gentleman in front of us was watching the scene and did not warn us that there was a large barrier at the top of our car and someone had to open the barrier gate in order to come inside the *'Caravan Site.'* We realised that this was not a certified *'Caravan Site'* but a place for the Irish Gypsies. When we walked out of the car, we could see the top of our caravan dented right in! We were extremely upset by this, and reversed our car back and joined the main road to head back to the North of Ireland.

Five Barking Dogs

As we were driving north towards Dublin, we were extremely tired and physically weak. We could not see a sign for a caravan site. Therefore, an alternative option was suggested by David.

1000 Years As One Day

He suggested that we should stay in a bed and breakfast (B&B) for the night and continue to drive up the following morning. Not long before he suggested this idea, Sarah had seen a B&B sign at the sharp turning on the right. David quickly turned the car and we were heading into a rural area once again. We could not turn the vehicle around, so we made our way to the end of the narrow road.

There was no vehicle passing by, no signs of people and it was an extremely quiet area. At the end of the road, we could see a large black metal gate with an intercom. David pulled the car near the intercom and pressed the buzzer. Then we could hear the Irish gentleman asking for the reason for our arrival at his gate. Sarah leaned over towards David and said out loud, *"We are looking for a B&B!"* Then there was a silence. The black automatic metal gate slowly opened. David slowly drove the car forward, making our way to the front of the large house door.

Missionary Journey in Republic of Ireland

An Irish gentleman in his 40s was standing in front of the house. He looked at us with a great suspicion. We wound down our car window and greeted the gentleman. Then the Irish gentleman said in a deep voice, *"There are no rooms available here."*

He was very unfriendly and then he shut the door on us. We were very disappointed by his behaviour and wound the car window back up. As soon as we turned the engine on to turn around the car, five large dogs were running towards our car! These dogs' eyes were like wolves and they were barking so loudly. Then all five dogs which looked like beasts were clutching their sharp claws on to our vehicle and we could see their sharp teeth, growling and saliva was dripping on to our car. They were ready to eat us alive!

They were like the five hungry lions or beasts which were capable of ripping apart human flesh into pieces. We were terrified and panicked, with our face turning red and sweaty face; our hearts beating extremely fast and crying to our Saviour for help. As David moved the vehicle close to the gate, the dogs were behind the caravan barking aggressively. Then the large black automatic metal gate opened slowly. We were in such a hurry to escape this haunted house. This was an unforgettable experience.

Missionary Journey in Republic of Ireland

Dublin - One-way system

We followed the sign to the North of Ireland and then the road we joined eventually merged into another road, which allowed us to step into the City of Dublin. We did not want to pass through this complex road, since it was operating on a one-way system and if we missed our turning, we would need to go around once again until we find a correct road which leads us back to the main road heading to Northern Ireland. To make the journey worse, we had the most severe down pour of rain. It was extremely dangerous, since the window wipers were not fast enough to keep the rain clear from the windscreen. We could not see where we were going and the Irish drivers were constantly *'Beeping'* from the back. We stepped into the one way system in a rush hour.

The road was extremely unsafe and we were crying and asking the Lord to deliver us from this place. After driving in circles for four consecutive hours in the rain, we joined the main road.

Our First Caravan and Fiat Vehicle - Northwich

Chapter 15

Missionary Journey in Northern Ireland

Religious Politics

As we passed through the border of Ireland and into Northern Ireland, we could see that the road signs were in English rather than Irish and English written on the same sign boards; the kilometres were changed to miles and the money was in pounds rather than Euros. We have witnessed a great division between Ireland and Northern Ireland. Furthermore, it was religion and politics which created that division, especially between the Catholics and Protestants. There was that reality of hurt and wounding in this environment.

Wall murals confirmed the history of these conflicts. It brought great sadness to see this situation in reality. In the past, Northern Ireland was known to have supplied many Christian Missionaries to other parts of the world and recognised to have a tradition based on a good witnesses of the Reformed Faith. We were indebted to God for the faithful work of Irish missionaries.

Lisburn Town Centre

Rather than taking us three hours, we drove around the country of Ireland six hours to reach the Ballynalich Road caravan site. We arrived at 3pm and did not have a sip of water. We were exhausted and needed much rest, nevertheless, as soon as we parked our caravan, we headed to the nearest Town of Lisburn.

Missionary Journey in Northern Ireland

As we arrived late at the Town Centre, we could not evangelise for long and later that evening we returned home. However, the following morning we visited the Town of Lisburn again. The Town Centre was great and we had an unbelievable response from the people. Two ladies were standing in the middle of the high street (as if they were paralysed) listening to our singing. Some people said, *"I could listen to you all day"* and refused to go home. That day we had to renew our car insurance. We needed to have that money lodged into our bank account and the Lord provided more than a double amount to cover our expenses.

Belfast Town Centre

Our next Town to visit was Belfast on a Sunday morning. Regretfully, we could see decline not dissimilar to other parts, where there was a falling away in belief and faith in Christian things.

1000 Years As One Day

Sadly, many people had less fear of God and were without hope in a troubled world. They did not know the joy and happiness of Christ in their lives and became submerged in the secular world of good and entertainment. Despite a lack of responses from the public, in Belfast, we continued to praise the name of the Lord in the main City Square. Then a gentleman came in front of us with a large professional camera, taking pictures of us evangelising. The photographer did not explain to us the reason he was taking pictures of us. After some time, we were in a different location, when we had found out that we were published in the newspaper of the year. 'The Irish News' on Friday 14th August 2009, we were featured on page 24. The photographer was Brendan Murphy and the subtitle of the photo was tagged, Songs of Praise: In Cornmarket, Belfast. We were so grateful to the Lord and to Brendan, who voluntarily made an effort to publicise us in that *'Catholic'* newspaper.

Missionary Journey in Northern Ireland

Andrew and Dorothy

There was a couple who lived three roads down from the Town of Larne. They opened their window in the morning, while having breakfast, and heard a sweet melody of the *'Old Rugged Cross'* hymn echoing down from the Town Centre. With a great surprise, Andrew hurried down to the Town Centre to see who was playing such a beautiful piece. At that time the weather was quite unpleasant. A severe down pour of rain and wind caused all our instruments to be wet and causing some damage to the electronic organ, guitar and the wooden recorder. Andrew had been observing our Ministry from a close distance. He said that Hannah was playing the electronic keyboard for five consecutive hours without a rest. With a great surprise, he took pictures of our family, recorded our music with his *'Old Cassette Tape'* and wrote a letter of appreciation. He later came back to give us a copy of the recorded tape with donations towards our Ministry.

We were so grateful for the Lord's provision and this encouraged us even more to travel around Northern Ireland to share the Gospel. The following week, we visited Larne Town again and as soon as Andrew heard the music, the couple ran out the house to meet us. Andrew and Dorothy were so pleased to see us again and he also testified the following, *"I felt there was a real magnet pulling us towards your family, the Lord's presence is with you and I can feel it."* He gave us another brown envelope, which he wanted to give us to use for the work of God. Andrew and Dorothy sell art work to support themselves, and they were not financially stable and yet their faith in the Lord was magnificent.

Not only did this couple supported us with finances, but they also brought us three packed lunches which consisted of sandwiches, cakes and soft drinks, which was a great help physically.

We could never forget their warm love, kindness and support they provided us during the time in Northern Ireland.

Ruth and Family

On a hot summer day, we visited Larne once again. At that time we were worried about finding a suitable caravan site. We prayed and asked the Lord to help us find a Christian who could help us. That morning, an elderly gentleman observed our Ministry work and had been greatly touched. He rushed home to speak to his daughter-in-law, Ruth. The elderly gentleman kindly asked Ruth if she could visit the Town in the afternoon to see the outreach which was happening in the Town Centre of Larne. Then Ruth drove to the Town of Larne to see a great number of people on either side of the road queuing up to speak to the musicians. These were the three folks which Ruth's father-in-law had spoken about.

Ruth joined the queue and once it was her turn, she asked where we were staying and how long we were here for. Sarah explained the following to Ruth, *"We are travelling various parts of Northern Ireland to share the Gospel. We were praying this morning to meet a Christian who could help us find a caravan site."* Ruth then replied, *"Come and stay with us!"* We then moved our caravan to their car park. Ruth had a lovely house which was built in a rural area outside Larne Town. They had a great automatic metal gate which opens as soon as the password had been inserted. As soon as the vehicle went through the gate, we come across a large area behind their house, where a caravan could easily be parked. They provided us with electricity connections as well as having access to the water outside their house. It was no different to a caravan site. Not only did they provide us with the space for the caravan, Ruth and family often invited us for dinner at their house.

Missionary Journey in Northern Ireland

They would often encourage us to use their house facilities in all circumstances. The whole families made us feel very welcome. One morning, Ruth had an idea about inviting her extended family to the house and having a praise and worship evening, followed by a meal. We thought this was a great idea and we promised to visit Ruth's home after the evangelism. As we arrived in the evening we met Ruth's aunt and uncle, and her parents as well as her mother-in-law and father-in-law. Ruth's husband and her three children were also there.

They had been looking forward to meeting our family. We all had a time of worship; while Ruth's father-in-law brought in a camera to take a video clip of the evening. After a time of great fellowship, Ruth's uncle took a professional photo of all the extended family and visitors. Later that week, Ruth's father-in-law brought a copy of the DVD with the group picture used as a cover of the front and back of DVD case. It was a lovely present and a memorable experience.

Last Day at Ruth's House

After staying at Ruth's house for ten days, we decided to head back to Preston, Lancashire. It was a lovely surprise when they bought us three tickets to Preston from Larne Harbour. They booked us a pre-paid breakfast as well, which we could enjoy on the ferry back to Preston. On our last day, we woke up 3.50am to catch the early ferry, and we were packing our belongings and attaching the caravan and car slowly, bearing in mind not to wake Ruth's family up in the early hours of morning. As soon as the automatic metal gate opened, Ruth rushed out in her nightgown and bare foot; she showed her tears and said, *"Wait! It was lovely meeting you, have a safe journey to Preston."*

Missionary Journey in Northern Ireland

Ruth had a great love towards missionaries and people who were doing the work of the Lord. The time of our fellowship with Ruth's family was unforgettable and it was so sad that we had to say goodbye.

The mission journeys with the caravan and car was a tremendous experience for the Choi Family and the Lord provided our every need to cover the cost. During the time we had been in Ireland and Northern Ireland, we travelled over 1,006miles (1,619km), visiting 13 Town Centres preaching the Gospel.

최창석 목사 가족이 3일 현재 출석하는 경기도 성남시 구미동 한생명교회 앞 공원에서 연주하
며 찬송을 부르고 있다.   성남=강민석 기자

Korean Newspaper Article - Seoul

Chapter 16

Mission Journey in South Korea

Amplifier Battery

The time came in 2008 spring time when our battery operated amplifier died on us during our open-air mission work in Lancashire, which was after the Caravan Mission Trip. Our amplifier was a key device to project David and Hannah's voice, singing hymns. We could not find such a device here in the UK. We purchased this great device back in South Korea. Therefore, it was our decision to head back to South Korea and look for the same device.

Since we immigrated to the UK in 1995, our family visited South Korea in the year 2000, 2006 and this was our third visit to the country. In the year 2000, we were extremely busy visiting extended family members. Nevertheless, in 2006 we dedicated a significant amount of time on the outreach work in Seoul and received quite a positive response from the public. We received support from Churches and extended family members. In 2008, as we were in South Korea again, we ought to continue with our mission work for the Lord. While it is important to visit extended family members, we thought that our priorities should solely focus on serving the Lord there.

One Life Presbyterian Church - Seoul

Back in 2006, we were sent as missionaries in the UK by a small Church called *'One Life Presbyterian Church.'* The senior Pastor Park supported us while in South Korea and promised that the financial support would be continued during the time we served in the UK. Nevertheless, we had lost contact and therefore we could not receive any regular donations from this Church. This made our Ministry work more challenging, nevertheless, the Lord sent *'angels'* to sustain the work of the Lord. Therefore, when we arrived in South Korea, we headed to *the 'One Life Presbyterian Church.'* That day the Senior Pastor Park was not at his office. Therefore, one of the assistant Pastors contacted him to say that the Choi Family arrived at the Church. Pastor Park was extremely surprised to hear this. When He came to the Church, he apologised about the lost contact and not being able to support us financially over the last two years. Pastor Park confessed that the Church size was decreasing in numbers. The financial condition was not stable and the Church leaders considered downsizing a number of missionaries which they were currently supporting. One missionary group they considered to downsize was the Choi Family Mission.

Since the Church did not have much information about the work of the Choi Family Mission; therefore, Pastor Park and his wife had a little disagreement with regard to this matter, and when the phone rang to say that the Choi Family Mission arrived at the *'One Life Presbyterian Church,'* it just struck Pastor Park. He thought that this was a warning from the Lord, not to downsize the Choi Family Mission. In the eyes of the Lord, they were very precious. Ever since that day, Pastor Park sent us two years' worth of mission donation into the bank account, provided us with the accommodation, a car, produced over 5,000 leaflets about our Ministry work and helped us to publish an article about the work of the Choi Family Mission in a well-known newspaper. It was quite unbelievable; the Lord recovered everything we suffered from in the last two years. Pastor Park introduced us to a few other Church meetings where we could take part and receive support.

Mission Journey in South Korea

Street Pastor in Busan

We then decided to depart to the Capital City of Seoul and to share the Gospel in Busan, which is a second most populous City. The drive lasted five hours, since the road was unfamiliar to us. There was a theology school in Busan, where they provided accommodation for us to stay during the time of our mission work. Busan Town was a rough place, where there was a significant amount of crime and fist fighting. We were surrounded by many poor communities; including alcoholics and homeless people. As we evangelised in Busan for the first time, we came across one short bald headed man, who looked quite tough and aggressive. He started to swear and disturb our evangelism. He called David over in order to have a little discussion. However, David kept looking to the Lord and continued to sing the hymns without rest. After half an hour of listening to the hymns, he became soft like a sheep, and came to us, and bought us three cold drinks. He had been touched by the Lord.

171

When we stopped and spoke to him, he said that he was also an Evangelist and it took him over 10 years to take a stand in the Town of Busan. There were many people who abused him and stopped him from evangelising. He showed his teeth and there were not many left. He explained that, because of a significant amount of fist fighting, he had lost most of his teeth. People now respect him as a street Pastor. He now takes care of the people in the street of Busan. His story was quite unbelievable.

At first, he did not know who we were and that was why he dealt with us brutally. He felt the Lord touching his soul as David was singing the old hymns. He felt that the Lord's Presence was with the Choi Family. We became friends and then he sat beside us and protected us during our evangelism in Busan. We also befriended a few alcoholics and homeless people who had been touched by the Singing Ministry.

It was quite an experience we have had during the time we were in Busan.

Phone Call

We were having a late lunch at a local Korean restaurant in Busan, when we heard Sarah's phone starting to ring. David's sister had rung to ask us where we were and what we were doing, as if she cared what we were doing for the Lord. This was quite a surprise and unexpected from her, since we knew of David's extended family and that they were not always caring or supportive in the work of the Choi Family. As soon as the phone call ended, David felt that we should head back to Seoul immediately. Hannah and Sarah did not question David but obeyed his order and packed our belongings and we rushed back to Seoul in the dark misty night.

1000 Years As One Day

David felt that there was something not right with the extended family circumstances and so the first place to visit was his father's home in Seoul. Late at night around 8pm, we knocked on the apartment door. There was no answer, Sarah shouted, *"Granddad! Open the door!"* After a while of waiting, a rough looking old man, who had not shaved or washed came out the apartment door and said in a weak trembling voice, *"Who is it?"* When Mr. Choi saw our family, he smiled and invited us into his apartment. The apartment was filthy, with a strange smell and the dinner table had rotten food and there was no sign of Mrs. Lee (David's mother). Sarah asked, *"Granddad, where is grandma?"* Mr. Choi replied, *"Your Aunty has taken away your grandma and she has not come back home for four months."* David and Hannah were not very pleased to hear this. Not one of the extended family members bothered to tell us about this circumstance. That evening, we cleaned some parts of the apartment and made room for us to sleep that evening.

Mission Journey in South Korea

The next day, we took Mr. Choi to the hospital for a check-up and he received medication and, because of his diabetes, Sarah made sure we had a machine to monitor Mr. Choi's sugar level. Three course meals were prepared by Hannah and she made sure that Mr. Choi had the appropriate meal to be in control his health and diet. David had taken care of his bathing; while Sarah shaved his beard and encouraged Mr. Choi to brush his teeth on a regular basis.

We did not realise that Mr. Choi had been abandoned for four months and was eating rotten food. David's little brother came from time to time to deliver the medications to Mr. Choi, but no one was there to help him regularly. Mr. Choi required daily attention. The medications David brother brought were piled in one corner and Mr. Choi did not take the medication. Due to this, his health deteriorated. Mr. Choi said the following, *"When I am asleep, my wife keeps appearing in my dream and I want to go and see her.*

1000 Years As One Day

Bring her back home." David heard his father's request and without a phone call to let his sister know we were coming, we dressed Mr. Choi smartly, and drove him to where Mrs. Lee was residing. When we rang the apartment bell David's sister saw her father outside her apartment door, she quickly opened the door. She was so surprised to see how her father had made his way to come to her apartment.

Mr. Choi was extremely pleased to see his wife and even though David's sister refused his mother to head back to Mr. Choi's apartment, Mrs. Lee packed her bags quickly and left her daughters apartment. Apparently, Mrs. Lee became sick and could not look after Mr. Choi and this was the reason why David's sister had taken her mother to her apartment. When we questioned her about Mr. Choi and why he was eating rotten food, and abandoned for four months, David's sister explained that this was David's younger brother's responsibility.

In fact, it was not one person's responsibility but everyone had their responsibility to look after their own father. No one cared for Mr. Choi or his health condition, and other extended families were too busy looking after their own family that they could not spare any time to care for Mr. Choi.

Hospital Care

We had the great responsibility to look after Mr. Choi's health. The *'Shin Ill hospital'* admitted Mr. Choi for three days. He was more seriously ill than we thought. He was on drips and had been monitored and checked by the medical Doctors. Hannah and David slept beside Mr. Choi's hospital bed over night in rotation. Mr. Choi was extremely grateful for the care and attention we had given him. Both Mr. Choi and Mrs. Lee were in and out of the hospital for check-ups and obtained medications.

After a month of care, Mr. Choi decided to follow David back to England and Mrs. Lee had no choice but to follow her husband's decision. There was great opposition from all our extended family members, but not one could provide an alternative solution. Since Mr. Choi did not want to be admitted to the care home in South Korea, he wanted to be in his apartment, but Mrs. Lee was too weak to look after her husband. Our extended family members could not dedicate time to look after Mr. Choi and Mrs. Lee. Therefore, despite the opposition, we all decided to pack up Mr. Choi's belongings and depart from South Korea permanently.

Departure to England

In August 2008, Mr. Choi had made a firm decision to leave his apartment and his children and leave South Korea for good. Mr. Choi's children cried and asked their father to stay in South Korea, but this did not deter Mr. Choi's decision.

At the airport, only two of his children and their family showed up to say goodbye to Mr. Choi and Mrs. Lee. Not all the extended family showed up at the airport. It was sad, since Mr. Choi may not have long life to come back to the main land and this might be the last chance to see their father, yet this did not concern them. Despite his health condition, Mr. Choi and Mrs. Lee were on the airplane for over 11 hours and safely landed in the land of Great Britain.

Caravan Site in Lancashire

We found a beautiful caravan site in Lancashire, where there were parks and lakes surrounded by green trees and birds. We stayed in this place, until we could find a more permanent place to live; we had to do our best to survive in the caravan environment. It was not an easy experience having to care for the elderly inside the caravan.

1000 Years As One Day

We had to understand how best to deal with Mr. Choi who had incontinence problems because of dementia. Mr. Choi would wake up in the middle of the night asking us to take him to the toilet, when he had the nappies on already, which was a big problem we had to face. This woke everyone up in the mornings, and brought frustration upon the family since they were unable to sleep. What is more, Mrs Lee had the issue with sleep disorder and would wander around the place during the night, without informing us where she was going. This concerned us significantly, and we found it hard to cope with this situation.

Daily, Hannah would carefully prepare three course Korean meals, inside the caravan with a small cooker. Sarah brought the water, using the 51 Litre water hog to roll the tank and was busy emptying the waste water. David had the responsibility to wash Mr. Choi daily and change his nappies and clothes.

Mission Journey in South Korea

Our family found it hard work caring for the elderly. Nevertheless, we felt that this was our duty to care for elderly. This was pleasing in the sight of our Lord. Mr. Choi enjoyed the lifestyle inside the caravan; he would smile every day because of the fact that he had family surrounding him every day. He was terrified in South Korea, the fact that the family members abandoned him for four months. Mrs. Lee on the other hand was not settling in a new environment and wished to return to South Korea. However, Mr. Choi requested to have his wife next to him and did not allow Mrs. Lee to head back to South Korea.

After the meal, Mr. Choi would sit on his wheel chair and ask us to take him to the lake, where there were English men attempting to catch fish. Mr. Choi enjoyed fishing in his youth and enjoying seeing people catching fish at the lake. One evening, as we pushed the wheelchair towards the lake, and Mr. Choi was very excited.

1000 Years As One Day

We had seen an English men holding in his arms one large salmon fish! Mr. Choi laughed and clapped and said, *"This man knows how to catch big fish!"* Little did Mr. Choi know that the Salmon fish had been dead for a while and this was floating on top of the lake, nevertheless this brought great happiness to Mr. Choi. Our full-time work was to care for the two elderly people. They required a full attention and we could not do any other job to sustain our living. This meant that there was no income for the household except what Mr. Choi brought over from South Korea. With his permission, we had to purchase expensive nappies for him, and suitable clothes and medication bought over from the counter (until we had a registered with a Doctor), insurance, fuel costs for the car, re-new road tax and purchased gas bottles for our caravan, and other caravan site fees (including accommodation fees). Mrs. Lee could not understand the amount of money it had cost the whole family in order to live in the United Kingdom.

She spoke negative reports to her husband saying, *"David had taken away all of your possessions and money and kept it for himself."* Mrs. Lee thought that the only reason we had brought Mr. Choi to the UK was because of his possessions. Therefore, she kept on complaining and making our lives very difficult. Mrs. Lee had always perceived David as seeking after money from his youth. Little did she know that David was a changed person, he was not concerned with Mr. Choi's assets. David confessed that, *"Even if my father did not have any assets or money, I would have still cared for him. This is my duty as a son."* Mrs. Lee did not believe David and consistently made a negative report to Mr. Choi.

Despite a negative report from Mrs. Lee, David's father Mr. Choi had no regret to follow his son David to the UK. Our family had good expectance to see Mr. Choi and Mrs. Lee surrender their lives to Jesus.

Our family wanted to see Mr. Choi and Mrs. Lee grow in their faith in the Lord Jesus Christ and have that deep relationship with Jesus before they depart this world.

Baptism of Mr. Choi and Mrs. Lee

Mr. Choi had always been conformed to this world, taking an interest in worldly politics, pop music, women and money. Mrs. Lee attended Church in her late 60s and prayed to the Lord for her husband's salvation. Twenty years later, Mr. Choi who was in his 80s decided to be baptised in the Church. The Pastor proceeded with his request and received a certification to prove that Mr. Choi had been baptised at the local Korean Church, yet Mr. Choi never attended Church Service after his baptism. Mrs. Lee and Mr. Choi did not approve of the idea of going to *'Hell'* if you don't believe in Jesus Christ.

That was the only reason for the baptism. Our family knew that Mr. Choi and Mrs. Lee were not practising Christians. They did not have that close relationship with Jesus. Therefore, David encouraged his parents to have evening house group Service every night in South Korea during his visit as well as when they both arrived in the United Kingdom. Time passed, and Mr. Choi had more desire to worship the Lord in the evening house group Service than Mrs. Lee.

One evening, Mr. Choi brought all the Bibles and hymn books all prepared for the Service in the evening. We were all so surprised, how the Lord started to change Mr. Choi's life around for Jesus. Mr. Choi's favourite hymn was *'Amazing Grace'* he cried and sang really loud every time we sung this piece together. When we talked to Mr. Choi about his past, he would repent of his sins to the Lord Jesus and asking the Lord for deliverance and grace.

1000 Years As One Day

Mr. Choi loved to pray *'The Lord's Prayer'* and to pray for his children. Every morning he woke up to have breakfast, he would pray and say the word *'A-men and A-men.'* We also had the opportunity to take Mr. Choi to the open-air evangelism work with his wife Mrs. Lee. While sitting comfortably in his wheel chair, he would distribute the Gospel tracts. Mrs. Lee would be less happy in doing the Lords' work, since she thought that it was embarrassing handing out leaflets in the Town Centre. Mr. Choi had always been the first person to distribute a great deal of Gospel tracts and often asked for more tracts from Mrs. Lee. He would shout *'Hallelujah!'* every time a person received Gospel tracts from him. The Lord was very pleased with Mr. Choi. We knew that Mr. Choi had given his whole life to the Lord Jesus. His dedication and love towards the Lord was maturing day-by-day.

After the evangelism, we had taken Mr. Choi and Mrs. Lee for a treat in McDonalds. This was Mr. Choi's favourite restaurant, especially the Fillet Fish burger, chips and tea. Every time we said to Mr. Choi *"Can you find the M sign, for McDonalds?"* He would point his finger and say *"Here it is!"* Then while parking the vehicle, he would read out loud *"The Lord's Prayer."* He was ready for his lunch. We had every confidence that Mr. Choi was ready for heaven and to see God face to face. On the other hand, Mrs. Lee, felt that not enough attention was given to her and she kept looking for ways to fly back to South Korea.

Run away

One morning while we were preparing the way to out to evangelise, Hannah said that Mrs. Lee was not well and she was sick in bed.

Sarah had taken breakfast to her and she ate extremely well and finished the whole meal. Mrs. Lee asked if she could stay at home, since she was not well. We all prayed for her and made sure that the back garden key was inserted - just in case of emergency, and there was plenty of food in the house. Little did we know that Mrs. Lee was deceiving us and made up her mind to run away from the house and fly back to South Korea. When we returned to the house, Mrs. Lee packed up her belongings, and had taken £350 worth of money and left the house. We searched for her all day, and could not find where she was. Mr. Choi was not pleased about this matter. In the evening we had a phone call from the police that she had taken a flight back to South Korea.

Death of Mr. Choi

Six months after Mrs. Lee abandoned her husband Mr. Choi, his health started to deteriorate. One morning, as David was washing Mr. Choi, he was extremely quiet and after he came out of the shower. David quickly went out of the bathroom to grab a towel; by the time he came back he had fallen and damaged his head quite severely. When David saw this he was extremely surprised, Mr. Choi could barely move. David held Mr. Choi in his arm and laid him on the bed.

We thought that he would recover the next day, so without any concerns we left Mr. Choi in his bed, allowed him to rest until the following morning. As Hannah and Sarah had taken the breakfast up in the morning and the medication, we held his hand and pulled him up to sit uprightly.

Hannah prayed for the food and the health recovery of Mr. Choi, and then he said, *"Amen."* As usual routine, Sarah gave the following tablets for his diabetes, blood pressure and aspirin tablet. Sarah put that medication in his mouth but Mr. Choi brought everything up. His eyes were rolling back and we all panicked. Sarah rang the emergency ambulance. They checked his pulse and quickly hurried him to the hospital.

Eventually after three days, Mr. Choi had gone into a coma and there was nothing we could do to keep him alive. We sat around his bed and nursed him, we also asked three senior Pastors to come and pray for his safe journey to Heaven. Each time we sang hymns and prayed we could see a great sunshine breaking through the hospital windows. Mr. Choi would sometimes open his eyes to see where his wife was, but we could not help him. Since the family would not allow us to speak to Mrs. Lee.

Mission Journey in South Korea

We visited Mr. Choi every day at the hospital, singing hymns and praying, While Sarah would clean Mr. Choi's mouth, and clean his neck, arms and legs. One morning, Sarah had seen her granddad's leg turning black and purple. This brought a great shock to our family. It was a sign that he was not long before he breathed his last breath. We came home and in the late evening around 11pm on Sunday, we had a phone call from the nurse that Mr. Choi had died. The nurse explained that there was a great breakthrough of sunshine as she entered the room, he looked peaceful and he held tightly on to the wooden cross when he passed away. Mr. Choi was in glory with the Lord Jesus.

Funeral Service of Mr. Choi

Our family made every effort to inform other members in the family about the death of Mr. Choi. We wanted the most peaceful funeral Service for Mr. Choi; nevertheless, his children did not cooperate with our family. One of David's sisters said, *"If our father is truly dead, then send us his body so that we may have a funeral Service here."* They had no respect for their father. We could not communicate with our extended family, as they were very unhelpful and aggressive towards our family.

Therefore, Sarah contacted the minister Timothy at the Minster Chapel in Preston, Lancashire with regard to organising Mr. Choi's funeral. This Church was one of the largest Churches in Preston Town Centre. The minister Timothy had also met Mr. Choi and knew of our family.

Mission Journey in South Korea

There were also Pastors from the local Churches supporting us with arranging the funeral Service. Sarah had never visited any funeral Services before and this was her first time organising one for her grandfather. David and Hannah could not help much but to pray that Christians would help Sarah in arranging the funeral Service. It was more complicated than what we had expected.

The flower arrangements, coffin, Service order, writing the Eulogy, photo of Mr. Choi and framing, finding a plot in the graveyard, stone for the graveyard and inviting members to attend the funeral Service as well as thanking them for the attendance. In January 2010, we held our main funeral Service at the Minster Chapel, Preston; followed by another Service at the Crematorium. The attendees of the main Service consisted of 70 members and 10 Ministers from various Churches to support our funeral Service.

Pastor Charles and the elder from the Church in Tamworth came to our house in the morning, on the day of the funeral Service. We were not expecting the members from Tamworth to come and support us. The distance from Tamworth to Preston was 216miles (348km) return journey. They must have travelled from early in the morning. We were extremely grateful and we had a great fellowship time with them in the afternoon. However, we were greatly saddened by a lack of cooperation from the extended family members back in South Korea. It was unfortunate that none of Mr. Choi's children and family made any effort to help with the funeral arrangements or to attend the funeral Service.

Mission Journey in South Korea

Burial for Mr. Choi

We kept Mr. Choi's ashes until we could find a suitable location for him. We did not want to bury him in a cemetery where various non-Christian people were buried there; we wanted Mr. Choi to be buried in a Church graveyard. We knew that this would be very difficult to achieve, since you had to be a member to be considered for a place in the Church graveyard. However, it was a miracle, when our family attended our local Church on Sunday morning, had our usual Holy Communion and Pastor Geoffrey asked us how we were coping and if there was anything he could do to help. Sarah mentioned that Mr. Choi's ashes were kept inside our house and we wanted to find a place to bury him. Then Pastor Geoffrey said, *"Come with me and let me show you our Church graveyard."* He said that there was one space at the back of the graveyard which would be perfect for Mr. Choi. Sarah asked, *"How could this be? It is very rare to find a space in the Church graveyard?"*

Pastor Geoffrey replied, *"We had a member who had recently died and we were supposed to bury her here but the coffin was too long for the space so the burial could not go ahead. However, your granddad's ashes could be buried here."* It was a miracle and the Lord was with us. Therefore, in July 2010, we held the 11am Service at the St. Michael Church for Mr. Choi's burial. Mr. Choi's life was extremely blessed at his last days. His grave stone reflects his faithfulness to the Lord, since *"His last word was A-men."*

Chapter 17

Mission Journey by Public Transports

Decision to Sell our Vehicle

The death of Mr. Choi had a great impact on David. Especially driving the same vehicle where his father was sitting beside him, made David feel very uncomfortable. Even visiting the same bathroom, where David washed his father daily and changed his clothes and nappy, this made him feel quite sad. Our family had been in absolute exhaustion dealing with Mr. Choi and Mrs. Lee. Caring for the elderly for two years, plus the caravan and car missionary journeys exhausted David mentally and physically to drive a vehicle around the United Kingdom. Therefore, we sold the car and have decided to use public transport to continue serving the Lord.

Sarah and Hannah's Education

During the time Sarah had taking care of her grandparents, she was accepted at Lancaster University to continue her studies. By the time Mr. Choi had passed away and Mrs. Lee moved back to South Korea, Sarah had been awarded a Masters of Science degree in Advanced Marketing Management at Lancaster University.

In addition, Hannah pursued her Theology studies during the time of taking care of Mr. Choi and Mrs. Lee. Hannah completed the prescribed formalities for a Theological Masters Degree through the Graduate Division of the General Assembly Theology Seminary. Moreover, Hannah was invited back to South Korea in order to receive the certification of ordination from the Presbyterian General Assembly, Theology Seminary of South Korea.

Mission Journey by Public Transports

Calling to Move away from Lancashire

When Sarah was in the process of completing the Master of Science degree at Lancaster University, she worked as a Marketing Executive in Technology based company. After two years of working at this place, it was time that Sarah moved on with her career. Therefore, our family made the decision to move away from Preston, in Lancashire. We opened the map and asked the Lord for the direction.

Then Sarah found a ticket online where a coach can drive from Preston Bus Station to London Victoria Bus Station. This must have been the same Bus route which Mrs. Lee had taken to make her way from Preston to London and then to Heathrow Airport and to South Korea. We had never taken a coach to London before and indeed this was a long journey. Nevertheless, we felt that Hannah had to travel back to South Korea in order to obtain her certificate of ordination.

1000 Years As One Day

Therefore, despite the long journey, we packed our bags and boarded the 2am coach from Preston to London. We first evangelised areas in London, covering the Towns of Brixton, Chelmsford, Colchester, Norwich, Clacton-on-Sea, Ipswich and South-end-on-Sea.

Then 11th July 2012, we booked airplane ticket for Hannah. Leaving at Heathrow at 8pm, we spent over £859 on the ticket, leaving David and Sarah only approximately £20 in the bank account. With great faith, Hannah departed from London, England to Seoul, South Korea. This was our first time we had been separated as a family. David and Sarah felt quite empty without Hannah. Nevertheless, we had to continue serving the Lord in the United Kingdom. Sarah knew that with £20, we could not travel back to Preston, and as we headed back to Ben's place (our Christian friend's house in London), Ben had prepared a donation for us to head back home. God was working miracles in our lives.

Mission Journey by Public Transports

As we went online and searched for the coach heading back to Preston, there were two tickets leaving from London at 3pm the next day. The money we had in our hand was the exact cost to get us to Preston. As we arrived in Preston early morning of 12am, we fell asleep at 12.20am at our home in Preston when Hannah called to say that she had safely arrived in Seoul, South Korea.

David and Sarah's Evangelism Journeys

When we arrived in Preston, Lancashire, we had a desire to pack all things and leave our belongings with a friend and then depart back to London. This was not an easy decision, since we had to clear out Mr. Choi's and Mrs. Lee's belongings, plus our family's belongings. The items were as much as four bedrooms which now had to be reduced to possessed one bedroom. David and Sarah were exhausted trying to clear out the household items.

1000 Years As One Day

We had a friend called Frank helping us to deliver our rubbish to the tip. Then while clearing, we accidently threw away all the important household documents as well. This included our passports, degree certificates and other important documents. David and Sarah sat on the floor of the empty room and asked the Lord for wisdom.

Since losing the important documents, Sarah was on the phone in order to obtain a copy of the degree certificate and then we visited the police station to obtain the right paper work with regard to the loss of our passports. Once a couple of issues were resolved, we were on the coach travelling back to London to carry on with the evangelistic work.

Mission Journey by Public Transports

London Bus and Luggage

David and Sarah were on the no. 250 Bus from Thornton Heath to Brixton. We had to take a large red suitcase, since we needed the keyboard to share the Gospel, accompanying David's singing. Along with a small round wheel bag which pulled the battery based amplifier, in order to project David's voice. We were both sitting at the back of the Bus when an African lady brought in a pushchair with a child. She could have easily parked the buggy beside our suitcase. However, this was not the case and she shouted down the Bus, *"Whose suitcase is this?!"* The whole Bus was silent, then she shouted again, *"Whose suitcase is this?!"* then the entire Bus passengers pointed their fingers towards us. The African lady said, *"Remove it now."*

We explained that it was too heavy to lift it to the top of the luggage space. Then the Bus driver refused to move the Bus unless the suitcase was removed from the wheel chair area. Eventually one strong man picked up our luggage and threw it on top of the luggage space, damaging our electronic keyboard. It was not easy taking our instruments to the Town Centre by public transport.

Barking in London

David and Sarah travelled by Bus early hours in the morning to reach the place called Barking in London. It was unfortunate to see that the roads were divided into two and significant amounts of traffic were passing by. There was a real difficulty trying to find a suitable and quiet place, where there were no cars rushing by. Then we came across a bench outside the Barking Train Station. There were a few shops in front of the bench.

Mission Journey by Public Transports

These shops may cause opposition we thought, nevertheless with limited options, we sat down and Sarah played the electronic organ while David played the guitar and sang hymns. Less than an hour had gone by we had an Indian gentleman who was the owner of the jewellery shop standing in front of us. He asked a question and we did not provide an answer.

We knew that he was not pleased with us being in front of his Business and that he came to make an objection. The owner of the Jewellery shop called two police officers. However, surprisingly, two authorities came to us and smiled, they were glad to hear such hymns echoing in the high street of Barking. One of the police officer suggested that we should move down the road and play our music by the Bus stop, since there will be no opposition at this place. In fact at this place where we were sitting, we could see that in front of us were the Headquarters of the Police Station.

When we arrived at the suggested place, we started to sing *"How Great Thou Art."* Then suddenly we could see the Chief Police Constable and fellow colleague officers *'stuck their head out the window'* listening attentively to the hymns sung by David. Every time the song finished, the police officers would clap loudly in order to encourage us. We had never encountered such an experience before. We shared the Gospel amongst the police force in London. Despite the opposition, we moved forward in faith and the Lord was with us and performed a miracle in that situation.

Barry - Wimbledon, South West London

On Sunday in the late afternoon, David and Sarah were really finding it hard to find a suitable place to stay in London. We could not ask our friend Ben again to help us with the accommodation.

Mission Journey by Public Transports

We tried one *'African Church'* in the morning, which was situated in Peckham and received a disappointing unfriendly welcome from the senior Pastor. Their Service was rather very strange, it must have been that prosperity Gospel Church. The whole Service was oriented towards the Pastor's wife's birthday celebration. During the Service, members of the congregations were bringing tithes and envelopes which were given to the Pastor and for a birthday present for 'mommy' which was referred to Pastor's wife. This really concerned David and Sarah, since this Church was not proclaiming the Gospel of Jesus Christ rather providing a wrong teaching and hindering members of the Church. The Lord had really opened our eyes by experiencing various types of Churches.

After spending a few hours in the morning in Peckham, we were on the Bus for hours without food, travelling aimlessly trying to find a place to sleep, to lie down for the night in order to carry on with our Ministry work for tomorrow.

1000 Years As One Day

We were extremely tired, and the day was beginning to darken. Then David had seen a light which was turned on at 8pm inside a chapel. We quickly rang the Bus bell and got off the Bus. We then crossed the road and walked inside the Church which was called *'All Saints.'* At that time, the preacher had spoken about providing hospitality to a stranger. Reading a passage from the Bible, Hebrews 13:2 *"Do not neglect to show hospitality to strangers, for by this some have entertained angels without knowing it."* It was not by coincidence that we had seen a light being turned on inside a chapel to hear such sermon as this. After the Service we told one of the congregation members about finding a place to stay for the night. The face of the congregation turned pale as we spoke of such circumstances. Indeed, hearing of the sermon might have been straightforward but putting that into practice was extremely difficult for the British Church congregation. One of the members quickly introduced us to Barry, since he was the one who preached on the subject of *'Hospitality.'*

Mission Journey by Public Transports

His face also turned pale but tried to force himself to smile, since the whole of the congregation watched him very carefully as to how he responded to this matter. Due to the eyes of the congregation, he had no choice but to take us to his home for that night. David and Sarah were grateful to the Lord and being able to use these circumstances to have deeper fellowship with the *'Leaders'* in the Church. Barry drove a black Audi Sports car and his house was situated in the heart of Wimbledon. This was the area for the rich communities. He had a three floor magnificent house with numerous empty guest rooms. He worked as a Finance Director and his wife was a Medical Doctor. We had been offered a cup of tea and biscuits and then Barry's wife showed us to the room where we were going to stay for the night. During that evening we did not see them coming out of their room. Next morning, we waited in the kitchen to say thank you and goodbye but they did not come out to greet us.

They must have been terrified of us staying at their place. We felt that despite of their intelligence and their position as the Church preacher, their level of faith was extremely low. Nevertheless, we still pray for all the people God led us to meet and that their faith may grow into maturity.

Cross Channel Service to Northern Ireland

David and Sarah could not travel around London unless there was a more long-term based accommodation was provided. Therefore, we contacted our friend Ben for his advice. Ben explained that he could not provide a space for us, because of the visitation of his extended family, there was no space in the house. However, Ben was extremely concerned and said, *"Look, leave your items in the house and search for a place, if you are really struggling then come back to us. We could possibly let you sleep in the living room."*

Mission Journey by Public Transports

We were extremely grateful and travelled on the Bus to search for accommodation. The day was beginning to darken and the time was 8pm, finding no accommodation in London. Therefore, David suggested that we ought to phone a lady called Emma in Northern Ireland, and see if she would welcome us to her flat for the time being. When we contacted Emma, she gladly invited us to her flat, providing the accommodation. Therefore, we hurried to the nearest *'Internet shop'* in order to book a Cross Channel ferry heading to Belfast in Northern Ireland from London Victoria. This Cross Channel Service ticket consisted of Bus travel from London Victoria to Stranraer and the Ferry to cross over from Stranraer in Scotland to Belfast in Northern Ireland. It was a long way around to reach Northern Ireland, but we had not investigated other easy routes to this place.

As we searched online, there was one departing at 11pm that evening. We had two hours to get to Ben's place in Thornton Heath and pick up our luggage then to quickly make our way to London Victoria Bus Station. Time was extremely tight but David said, *"We can make it don't worry."* So we took the taxi. While we were inside the vehicle, Sarah phoned Ben and asked him to bring the luggage outside the house for collection. Ben asked, *"Have you found a place?"* Sarah replied, *"We are heading to Northern Ireland tonight and we only have less than two hours left to reach London Victoria Bus Station."* Ben was extremely surprised by our faith and determination towards Jesus. When we approached at Ben's place he had the suitcase ready for collection. We said our goodbyes and then rushed to the Bus Station. We just made it to the Bus heading from London to Stranraer which was 421miles (678km) and 7 hours 22 minutes Bus journey to Southwest Scotland.

Mission Journey by Public Transports

The accommodation for that evening was sleeping on the Bus, travelling hundreds of miles without stopping, water or food. We were extremely exhausted but we knew that this was an opening from the Lord.

A few years later we found out that there was no record of such Cross Channel Service for 11pm. This was a special occasion which the Lord shown us in the time of trouble. We had been in Northern Ireland and Republic of Ireland at two occasions. In 2007 and 2009, this was our third time we were heading back to Northern Ireland to share the Gospel.

"I have set the Lord always before me. Because He is at my right hand, I will not be shaken. Therfore my heart is glad and my toungue rejoices; my body also will rest secure, because you will not abandon me to the grave, nor will you let your Holy One decay, You have made known to me the path of life; you will fill me with joy in your presence, with eternal pleasures at your right hand."

(Psalms 16: 8-11 NIV)

Chapter 18

Moving to Northern Ireland

Meeting Emma - Ballymoney in Northern Ireland

After 7 hours 22 minutes journey from London to Stranraer, then three hours ferry journey from Stranraer to Belfast, David and Sarah finally arrived in the land of Northern Ireland. It was a long tiring journey, yet there was more travelling to do. We had to take the train from Belfast to Ballymoney which was 1 hour 35 minutes journey on the train. Due to a lack of food, we kept falling asleep on the train, it was a very tiresome journey and we really needed comfortable and warm hospitality.

1000 Years As One Day

When we arrived in Ballymoney, Emma brought her little car and greeted us at the Train Station Car Park. She gave us a hug and said, *"It is really good to see you again."* We met Emma few years before in Coleraine Town Centre during our evangelism. Emma really appreciated the work we were doing for the Lord. Emma provided accommodation for us and introduced us to several friends in Northern Ireland. When we visited Emma's friend's house, we were taking part in their prayer meeting and David was able to preach the Word of God to them. Our family has a great memory of the fellowship we had with Emma and her friends. The experience and memory of Northern Ireland was extremely positive during our mission journeys back in 2007 and 2009. When we first met Emma, she explained her circumstances to us with regard to her married life. She suffered from a divorce and lived as a single mum raising two children by herself. There were many times we came to the Lord in prayer for Emma's future life and her children.

Moving to Northern Ireland

Due to her circumstances, she lived in a council house, which was owned by the government. This meant that the visitors can only stay for few nights. Even though she had an empty guest room, we were not allowed to stay for long. This meant that David and Sarah had to keep searching for their own accommodation.

Rachel and Ian - Portstewart in Northern Ireland

There with few people helping us to find a suitable place to stay, David and Sarah met a couple called Rachel and Ian. It was our first time of meeting them both, and we were so grateful for their offer in providing the accommodation for David and Sarah. When we arrived at their five bedroom bungalow property, the place looked quite empty with very little household items inside.

1000 Years As One Day

Rachel explained the following, *"Ian and I only had been married for a year and we only recently moved into this property, so we are not settled yet. But you are very welcome to stay here."* We were so grateful for their kindness and the room was extremely spacious, we had our own bathroom upstairs, while Rachel and Ian had their own bathroom inside their room. The living room had a fire which was extremely warm and comfortable. Opposite the living room, there was another room where they had the dinner table and an old wooden piano. Sarah sat on the piano chair and started to play the old hymns. Then David started to sing praises to the Lord, soon Rachel and Ian joined in with us as we sang together. The bungalow turned into a Church. As we were worshiping the Lord, Rachel called her friends, inviting them to come over and meet David and Sarah. Consequently on the first day we had our worship Service at Rachel and Ian's bungalow, with her friend Alison, Alan, Paul and Sharon.

Moving to Northern Ireland

During the time of worship, David and Sarah had the opportunity to share a story about the Choi Family Mission journeys and had a time studying the Word of God. That evening, we sat around the table, and had a lovely meal and cup of tea and biscuits.

Rachel introduced us to her brother Paul and his wife Sharon. They helped us with the transport, from Rachel's place in Portstewart to Coleraine. Since the transportation in Northern Ireland was expensive and Buses were less frequent in comparison to London. A vehicle was required in order to travel freely in Northern Ireland. Due to David being unable to drive, we had to rely on the other Paul and Sharon's vehicle to move around several Towns in Northern Ireland to share the Gospel. After the morning evangelism, when we arrived at Rachel and Ian's place, we had evening prayer meetings with around eight people attending. David prepared the sermon and Sarah led the music.

It was wonderful to see a group of people lifting high the name of Jesus. Having that true fellowship in Jesus and caring for each other, praying for one and another. A few weeks later we also met Ian's parents.

They came to visit Ian and Rachel. Ian's parents enjoyed singing hymns, so after having lunch together at Rachel's place, we had a time of worship. As time passed by, more people were attending our prayer meetings in the evening. The numbers increased to about twelve. It was important to have refreshments after the Service. However, we did not realise that the preparation of the food for each evening would be so costly. Therefore during our prayer meetings, we came to an agreement to do a little collection in order to purchase food for the evenings. We then allocated a treasurer which was Ian, Rachel's husband.

Moving to Northern Ireland

The prayer meeting flourished and the activities had been increased to evangelising in the open-air during the Sunday evenings at the Portstewart Crescent bandstand. Some of the group members came together at the Portstewart Crescent Bandstand on Sunday evenings at 8pm and we all sang hymns, preaching the Gospel to the people who were walking pass. Portstewart Crescent Bandstand is located at a seaside resort, neighbouring Portrush Town in Northern Ireland.

This place previously had a variety of events and popular groups have performed music and dance at this place. As we were sharing the Gospel, we had a couple of bikers stopping by and listening to the sermons. It was a great evening witnessing for the Lord Jesus.

Enniskillen - Northern Ireland

After evangelising local Towns in Northern Ireland, David prayed about evangelising elsewhere. He felt that the Lord was directing him to Enniskillen. We informed this to Rachel and Ian, and then Paul and Sharon insisted that they would help us by taking us to Coleraine Bus Station. Subsequently, David and Sarah departed from Coleraine to Belfast on a Saturday morning. By the time we arrived at Belfast Bus Station, it was already 11am. Then we waited for x261 Bus heading to Enniskillen, the journey lasting an additional two hours. When we arrived at the Town of Enniskillen, it was 1pm. As we were singing hymns and sharing the Gospel, there was a down pour of rain, so we quickly looked for a shelter. There was a bandstand set up in front of us. There was no one performing inside this bandstand. We did not know who to contact in order to obtain permission.

Moving to Northern Ireland

Therefore, David and Sarah took a deep breath and stood inside the bandstand. It was a great cover for the instruments and we were able to sing freely without getting wet from the rain. David and Sarah did not realise that the time was quickly rushing by and that the last Bus to leave Enniskillen to Belfast was at 6pm. We had been singing in the afternoon for 4 hours without a break. David and Sarah therefore finished the evangelism around 5pm then headed to a local café shop to have a light late lunch. When we finished the meal and rested a little while, we made our way to the Bus Station at 7pm. There were no Buses and the Bus stop time table did not indicate when the next departure was.

One gentleman said that there will be no more Buses for tonight and the next one will be at 8am the following morning. We did not know anyone in Enniskillen, no contact, no friends. The day was beginning to darken.

1000 Years As One Day

We waited an hour in the cold outside the Bus Station and feeling hopeless. Then David saw a gentleman with a dog. David said that this gentleman had seen us evangelising at the bandstand this early afternoon. He was intensively listening to our singing. With delight and having some hope, Sarah approached the gentleman. Sarah said, *"Sorry to bother you sir, but we did not realise that the last Bus to depart back to Belfast was at 6pm and the next Bus will not arrive at this Bus Station until the following morning at 8am. We need to stay somewhere for tonight but we do not know anyone here in Enniskillen. Can you please help us?"* The gentleman looked at Sarah very seriously and said, *"Wait here, I would need to walk back home to bring my car and then we can have a drive around Enniskillen to find a place for you to stay for the night."*

Moving to Northern Ireland

The gentleman was called Tony and lived in Enniskillen for most of his life and he knew of some friends who might help. It was a dark cold night and with heavy rain, and as we approached Tony's friend's house, the house lights were all turned off. It was too late in the evening, so Tony reversed the car and then drove 3miles (5km) down the road.

When we approached this house, the living room light was turned on. Then Tony walked out of the car and knocked on the door. A lady called Esther answered the door and greeted Tony. As he explained the situation, Esther explained the following, *"As you are aware, my husband is not so well and I only have a single room. I cannot take two people but only one person at my house and then possibly my mother, Jean could take the other person, she is only down the road from me and since she has an empty single room, she would be able to accommodate."* That was the plan, however David felt very nervous sending Sarah into an unknown place.

There was no alternative option. David stayed with Esther and Sarah stayed with Jean. Then Tony said the following, *"Have a good night's sleep and I will come and pick you up 7.50am to take you to the Bus Station."* When David entered into the house, Esther asked David to pray for her husband. So David earnestly prayed for the husband of Esther. Subsequently, Esther wrote a note in the morning and passed it to David. Inside the letter, Esther had inserted a Bus fare to head back to Coleraine and said, *"Thank you David for your prayers. Your love is great."* Sarah stayed with Jean and befriended a widowed elderly lady. Jean had taken care of Sarah in the evening, providing a warm comfortable bed and lovely breakfast in the morning. They had a time of prayer and a great time of fellowship. Then Tony knocked on the Jean's front door at 7.45am to pick up Sarah and then headed to Esther's place to pick David up from the house. Then we headed to the Bus Station.

Moving to Northern Ireland

We had not known a single person in Enniskillen and yet the Lord led us to meet three wonderful people. We could not thank them enough for their kindness and generosity. Above all, we thanked the Lord for being with us and taking care of us in this situation.

Rachel and Ian's Problem

It had been a month since we stayed with Rachel and Ian. One day, as David and Sarah came back from the evangelism; we opened the front door and could hear a sound of crying. Rachel was on the floor in her living room crying. Sarah said, *"What happened Rachel? Why are you crying?"* Rachel explained the following, *"I only wanted to live a normal happy life, and so I decided to marry Ian. Look Sarah, I had been divorced once, my previous husband had been beating and torturing me, abusing me, assaulting me.*

I have a teenager daughter and she does not want to live with me anymore. Then I met a handsome looking man, Ian, I thought he was the perfect man for me. However, I had found out that Ian has problems too. He had been married before, but no children. He had been serving the Country for 18 years as an Army Officer, and he is not mentally well. He kicks and shouts during the night, visualising bombs and dead bodies. He had been involved with the Iraqi war, and this had tortured him. He has drinking problems, and he has taken all of our savings. We need to pay our £600 rent. He has taken all of that and the money we collected at the prayer meeting. I think there was around £23 in that pot. I don't know where he is."

Sarah tried to calm Rachel down and David had a time of prayer with her. The police were looking for Ian, and searching all around Northern Ireland for him. David and Sarah did not know what to do in this situation. We never knew that Rachel and Ian had a significant amount of suffering and hurt from the past.

Rachel had not been eating for a few days. Therefore, Sarah suggested cooking lovely meal of Rachel's favourite Spaghetti Bolognese; and have a time of prayer. Rachel, Paul and Sharon, Sarah and David sat around the dinner table inside the kitchen, gave thanks and ate the meal. Sharon prepared some trifles and cream for dessert. It was a lovely evening meal and Rachel was enjoying her dinner. Then we heard shouting behind the kitchen window. Rachel stood up and said, *"It's Ian! It's Ian! He is back!"* Ian came to the front of the house and started to be aggressive towards Paul and Sharon, kicking their car tyres. Sarah could see that Ian had drunk a significant amount of alcohol. It was dangerous, and Sharon quickly rang the police for assistance. Rachel said, *"I need to go and speak to him."* Sarah hid the front door keys and said to Rachel, *"It's too risky, don't go outside, and wait until the police arrive."* Despite the warning, Rachel used the garage door to escape the house.

1000 Years As One Day

Paul and Sharon ran outside and went inside the car and drove off to their house as well. It was just David and Sarah, in an empty haunted house with a garage door half opened. It was very dark and misty, we were extremely terrified. So Sarah said, *"Dad, let's pack our bags and go elsewhere."* David said, *"We cannot leave Rachel alone here. We will have to wait until Rachel tells us to leave."* So Sarah tightly held on to her father's arm and walked slowly to the local Tesco Supermarket.

As we were walking, Sarah's phone started to ring. It was Helen, Sarah's good Christian friend from Lancashire. It was very rare for her to ring at this time. Sarah answered the phone with a startling voice. Helen said, *"Hi Sarah! I was meaning to call you for ages and never had a chance to call you back. We are missing you so much in Lancashire. How are you?"* It was so lovely to hear Helen's voice in the midst of this frightening situation.

Moving to Northern Ireland

Sarah explained what had happened in Portstewart Northern Ireland that evening and Helen kindly offered to pray with Sarah over the phone. Once the phone call ended, we were heading back to the bungalow. Then we saw the police car, with Rachel inside the vehicle. The police explained that Rachel had to be admitted to a hospital for a check-up. Since, Ian had hit her head and caused an injury. Therefore, David and Sarah made their way to the hospital with Rachel and stayed there until 3am. We then made our way to Rachel's house again.

Sarah made a call to Joanna, a friend of Emma, who lived in Portrush. Joanna kindly offered to come over to Rachel's bungalow to check the safety of the house. Joanna walked upstairs to check three bedrooms, a bathroom and then the kitchen, lounge, and living room. As well as the garden, and garage. Joanna said, *"You are safe, don't worry."*

David and Sarah went into their room, and put knives and forks under their bedroom door, to prevent anyone from entering the room during the night and slept. The Lord was with us in this horrifying situation.

The following morning we entered the kitchen and saw that a few of the items were missing. Then Alison (a friend of Rachel's) who told us that Rachel is moving out of this property. Later that week, Rachel said, *"We have the house until the end of this month. You are welcome to stay here until then. But it is time that you guys go your way and I go my way."* David and Sarah were so glad to hear this. We had the freedom to leave this haunted place. David and Sarah had come to know that there was a lot of family abuse, marriage abuse and physical and mentally ill people in Northern Ireland. A significant amount of healing and prayer was required.

Sharon's Eye Damage

There was one occasion when we saw domestic violence for the first time. In the evening around 10pm, Sharon called into Rachel's house. Sharon called Rachel and she had taken Sharon to the kitchen and turned on the light. Rachel screamed and called, *"David, David and Sarah come and have a look at this!"* with a great shock, Sarah called the ambulance. Sharon was covered in blood with her left eye being seriously damaged.

Rachel said, *"Who did this to you Sharon, tell me!"* Sharon Said, *"Who do you think? It's my husband Paul, we were arguing over attending a Church meeting and he grabbed my hair and pinned me to the wall and with his fist..."* Sharon cried. Rachel said, *"That's it, I will have serious dealings with him. He cannot do this to a woman."* The ambulance arrived to admit Sharon to the hospital and we all went inside the ambulance with Sharon to the hospital.

We were asked to remain at the waiting room until further notice. It was 4am in the morning without any sign from the Doctors, so we called a taxi to head back home to Rachel's. Sharon's husband had a serious mental illness which caused him to behave such way, being out of control. Sharon suffered a significant amount of hurt and sadness from the marriage. Later that year, Paul and Sharon were divorced, because of being unsafe in that environment.

Prayer Meeting

While we were looking for accommodation, David and Sarah contacted Sophie who was a friend of Emma. She offered to help us with accommodation. While at Sophie's place, we met her children; they were all in their 30s, married with children. We came to know that Sophie was a single mum raising four children. Moreover, one of Sophie's children was a single mum also raising seven children.

Moving to Northern Ireland

Most of the people we had come to know were single mums who had a terrifying marriage life. Some of them were re-married but still finding no happiness. We had the opportunity to start the prayer meeting once again with Emma, Joanna, Sophie and her children. We had nine people attending house group meetings, praying for each other and the country of Northern Ireland. During the prayer meeting, Sophie had raised an issue with regard to her stomach pain. She had been suffering for nearly 20 years. We all prayed for her and later, after a few weeks, she said that the pain had gone and now she could sleep peacefully. The Lord was working miracles in Northern Ireland.

Moving House to Circular Road in Coleraine

Sophie's house was extremely comfortable for David and Sarah. Due to Sophie's circumstances of living in a council government property, we could not stay there for a lengthy time. Sophie had brought a newspaper one day and asked us to see if there were properties we could find for a long-term purpose. Then Sarah came across a private landlord's mobile number, the advertisement stated that there was a one bedroom property available for rent, in Coleraine. Therefore, Sarah made the enquiry and the landlord suggested meeting at the Railway Road in Coleraine the next day.

The landlord we met was called Jack, he showed us the property, yet we were not fond of this place. Sarah asked a question, *"Jack, do you have another property?"* He said, *"You don't like this place? Well I have one in Circular Road.*

Moving to Northern Ireland

I can take you there now and show it to you, if you want?" We all agreed to view another property. This place was better than the previous flat. It was a ground floor one bedroom but very spacious. It was located near the Town Centre of Coleraine and a short distance walk to the Train and Bus Station. It was ideal for travelling and to evangelise in various areas in Northern Ireland. Jack then had taken us to his business, down the road from Circular Road. He said, *"I own this place, and have been doing business for over 26 years. If you were to take the flat in Circular Road, you can come and see me at any time, if you have any issue. I will be close by to help you but I know you will not have much issue with this place; the tenants are pretty well behaved. Also, there is another flat above my shop. It is a better place but it is not vacant at the moment. I could let you know when it becomes vacant."* Jack was extremely kind to us. We signed the contract to the flat in Circular road and Jack gave us permission to move in the following day.

1000 Years As One Day

We were extremely happy to have our own place and the fact that we did not have to move every three days to different locations. Finally, we were able to settle down and bring our household items from Preston in Lancashire. When we went back to Sophie's place and told her that we were moving to our own flat in Coleraine, Sophie was extremely pleased. She offered to help with transporting our luggage to the new flat. Sophie said, *"Is there anything you need at your new flat?"* Sarah said, *"We need some duvets, pillows and bed sheets."* Sophie contacted few of her friends and brought two double duvets and two pillows with bed sheets.

When we moved into the new flat the next day, we visited a couple, Naomi and Glen. We met them at the evangelism in Coleraine. Naomi prepared tomato soup and sandwiches last time we met them. They lived not far from Circular Road.

Moving to Northern Ireland

As soon as Sarah mentioned that the Choi Family moved to Circular Road, Naomi said, *"Right, there must be household items you need for that place. Come with me and I will supply them for you."* We were so grateful; few Christian friends helped us to be settled into our new place and we did not have to bring our household items from Lancashire in a hurry, since we had most fundamental necessary items being all prepared for us. The Lord was with us and helping us to start a new life in Northern Ireland.

Donald - Eye surgeon

Our family made a good friend with Pastor Donald since we were living in Preston, Lancashire. We met him when we were invited to the Church in Lancashire. Pastor Donald is a humble and faithful Christian, who works in the Church as a Pastor, and as a profession he is an eye surgeon.

1000 Years As One Day

When we met him, he was greatly touched by our Ministry and since we met him for the first time, he had been making a significant amount of contributions towards the Choi Family Ministry. When we arrived in Northern Ireland, Pastor Donald had been generously paying for 24 items of foods from the local supermarket and making sure that it arrived at our home on time.

In most cases, when we depart our home to evangelise in Southern Ireland or England, we had to always empty our fridge (preventing food from decaying). Therefore, when we have arrived at home, Pastor Donald had made the online orders on time, so that we would always have our necessities when we arrive at our home. Also, when we had run out of our travelling fees, Pastor Donald sent the exact money to cover the cost of travel.

Moving to Northern Ireland

For example, we had ten Town Centres which we had the desire to visit, but it was too far of a distance from home that we could not reach these places unless we had a great amount of donations to cover this cost. Pastor Donald had been a key contact and supporter where he had given so much for the work of God. The Choi Family Ministry would not have been sustained if it wasn't for Pastor Donald. We thank God for him and his life.

"Though I walk in the midst of trouble, You preserve my life; You stretch out your hand against the anger of my foes, with Your right hand You save me."
(Psalms 138:7)

Chapter 19

Higher Education

Doctor of Philosophy Degree

David and Sarah were travelling on the bus from Coleraine to Portrush, while staying with Rachel and Ian. When passing through, there was a great large building and David and Sarah had never intended to question what type of building it was. Then one day, David had seen a sign post which had stated, *"The University of Ulster"* written on the way to the entrance. David had always mentioned that it would be good for Sarah to take up the Doctor of philosophy (PhD) degree, since David always desired to pursue his education, yet failed to succeed.

1000 Years As One Day

With God's help, Sarah achieved greatly and for His glory it was good to pursue a further higher education. David and Hannah did not have the money to support Sarah financially for the three years of Doctoral degree course, yet with faith, Sarah made an enquiry to the person in charge at the University of Ulster. It was a real surprise when we received an email so quickly from the professor at the University of Ulster.

He was in charge of the Doctoral degree course, and advised that a supervisor had to be chosen from a list on the website and contact the selected academic directly. From the website list, there was a suitable lecturer in the field of social media for business. Sarah made the contact and a few days later, the University lecturer contacted Sarah and requested to meet up for a short discussion with regard to the application procedures and to answer any questions with regard to the admission process.

Higher Education

Sarah had been wearing the same clothes for the last four months, doing open-air mission with David. Sarah was quite embarrassed to walk inside the University building wearing the old rugged clothes. This type of clothes was suitable for doing the open-air mission, especially being surrounded by alcoholics or homeless people but not for a University meeting. Sarah was urgently waiting and praying for the household items from Lancashire to arrive in Circular Road prior to the meeting with the lecturer at the University of Ulster. Amazingly the clothes and the household items arrived a day before the meeting appointment. The only item Sarah needed was that long expensive brown and black woollen coat, which Sarah had worn at the place when she worked professionally in Blackburn. When she ironed the coat and worn it, no one could have known that she had been working in the open-air pastoring the homeless and alcoholics. Sarah was ready for a meeting with the academic at the University building.

The first meeting with the lecturer had been successful and during the meeting with that lecturer, he suggested that a second supervisor should also be selected. He advised that a few additional supervisors for support were necessity. At the second meeting at the University of Ulster, Sarah had the opportunity to meet a female lecturer. They both were keen to help Sarah to be admitted as a PhD student at the University of Ulster. After a long discussion and a month later, Sarah submitted a draft paper of the PhD research proposal. Both of the lecturers were delighted with the outcome and helped Sarah with the application process. During the conversation, they mentioned that the proposal which was submitted was good enough to receive a scholarship. Then we all pursued the application and waited to hear the outcome from the University. A few months later, Sarah had a letter which stated the interview date.

Higher Education

After attending the interview, another letter came through the post to indicate that Sarah was on the waiting list to be considered as a fully funded PhD student. Then later that year, a phone call was received indicating that Sarah received the scholarship to study at the University of Ulster as a PhD student. Sarah never received school or University scholarships before and in order to receive the scholarship award, the applicant to be an outstanding performer with exceptional intelligence above the norm. The application process at the University of Ulster was very competitive and less than 10 people were selected out of 160 applicants to be a fully funded PhD student. Sarah earnestly prayed to the Lord and repeated the scripture verse of Philippians 4:13 *"I can do all things through Christ who strengthens me."* Indeed, the Lord performed a miracle in Sarah's life. Sarah was so grateful to the Lord for his love, grace and mercy. She had five months to prepare for her PhD admission in September.

1000 Years As One Day

Sarah was extremely pleased with the outcome, therefore, as thanks and gratitude to the Lord, she dedicated that five months to the Lord by travelling around Ireland and England to share the Gospel of Jesus Christ. The year Sarah was admitted at to Ulster University, she had been travelling with her father David to 56 Town Centres, in Northern Ireland, Republic of Ireland and England (including Birmingham and London areas). During that time Sarah had the opportunity to counsel and pray for people, leading the following people to Jesus; Frank (alcoholic), Maureen, Terry, Malcolm (drug addict), Agi, Margaret, Lynda, Rachel (80 years old lady) and Timothy. While people were turning to Jesus, Sarah and David also had the opportunity to pray for people.

The following people reported that after the prayer, the Lord healed their diseases; Margaret healed from suffering great pain because of her black toes and swollen feet, Jack healed from sleeping disorder, Paul healed from migraines which lasted for six months and Jack healed from blurred vision because of a cataract in one eye. The Lord was showing miracles that year during the mission trips.

Teaching Opportunities

During the summer, Sarah had the opportunity to do some freelance teaching jobs. Since there was a lack of Korean people living in Northern Ireland, the company based in Belfast contacted Sarah and asked her to deliver a structured language and cultural awareness tuition programme to a group of local business men to support their marketing initiatives in South Korea.

In addition to this opportunity, the lecturer from the University of Ulster asked Sarah to deliver six weeks of lectures to a group of Undergraduate students. Modules covering the areas of: communication marketing, consumer behaviour and consumer marketing management. Sarah received a positive feedback from the students. Sarah was able to shape the future of marketers by guiding them through their higher education processes. Sarah had the opportunity to see a group of Undergraduate students (which she taught for six weeks) walking down the stage and receiving their Bachelor's degree award.

Sarah always desired to have a caring, compassionate lecturer, yet this was never achieved. Then one day, the Lord reminded Sarah the following, *"You need to be that lecturer which you desired."* The Lord was directing Sarah, asking her to give that Christian care, love and compassion which other lecturers were not giving.

Higher Education

Sarah developed a good working relationship with students. At the end of six weeks of teaching, one student wrote the following comment: *"Sarah Choi is a fantastic lecturer who takes personal interest in her students and goes above and beyond to help them. She is very knowledgeable about her subject and is incredibly reliable and consistent! I wish her all the best in her career as she is a hardworking, diligent, caring person with much to give to her field."*

Sarah had a great opportunity at the University of Ulster being able to provide feedback and enhance students learning. As the time passed on, a few more lecturers from various departments requested Sarah to teach on the subject of employability and marketing. Sarah had the opportunity to teach first to third year Bachelor's degree students and MBA business students. The feedback had always been positive from the students and lecturers alike.

After two years of being a Doctoral Candidate, Sarah had the opportunity to deliver a talk on the subject of "Harnessing the power of social media to leverage maximum business potential" to a group of Chief Executive Officers in Northern Ireland. In the University of Ulster, Sarah was the first PhD student to take up this opportunity. Sarah was the first South Korean PhD student within the University of Ulster to pursue this opportunity. This was the most successful achievement that the Lord had given Sarah.

Prestigious Conferences

During the time as a Doctoral Researcher at the University of Ulster, Sarah had the opportunity to present her research findings at prestigious conferences. Sarah presented her research at the British Academy of Management Conference in September 2014, and then at the Academy of Marketing Conference in July 2015.

Higher Education

At these conferences, thousands of Doctoral students around the world apply in order to present their research findings, receiving feedback from the well-known professors around the world. It is a very competitive process and only few can be chosen within the individual University Institution. The research paper had to be exceptionally well written and presented. There was a rigorous peered-review feedback, where a research paper is submitted and then passed on to individual academics within the field of expertise. Then the lecturer gives critical feedback which the applicant must address before re-submitting the final piece of the document.

Once this complicated procedure is handled, then the conference team allocates a time where the researcher must attend to present the paper. It was a life time experience for Sarah. She was the first South Korean PhD student within the University of Ulster to be chosen to present her research paper at the prestigious conferences.

Following on from the conference, Sarah had a request from SAGE publications, asking her to publish her research paper with them. They asked Sarah to write a business case study which could be published at their Business Knowledge series. Again, this was a great success which the Lord had given Sarah. Later in March 2016, Sarah had published for the first time with SAGE publications. The Lord transformed Sarah from nothing to something. She had no intelligence to even pass her high school exams, yet the Lord had made Sarah into an author, public speaker and University Lecturer. At this time, Sarah desired nothing more from the Lord, since He answered every prayer, and accomplished everything which Sarah asked for. The Bible says, *"And keep the charge of the Lord your God; to walk in His ways, to keep His statutes, His commandments, His judgements, and His testimonies, as it is written in the Law of Moses that you may prosper in all that you do and wherever you turn."* (1Kings 2:3 NKJV)

Chapter 20

Unforgettable Year

House Move

In 2015, the Choi Family moved to Park street, a two bedroom property which is located in the heart of Coleraine Town Centre (Northern Ireland), near the pedestrian zone of the Town. Park street had 13 properties which were red brick mid-terrace houses. Mostly the residents were elderly and privately owned. It was an extremely safe environment for our family and this was the best property we lived in within those 20 years of living in the Great Britain. It was a miracle as to how we managed to move into such an amazing place and location.

1000 Years As One Day

Our family moved house every year before, being unsettled at all times and always staying with other tenants in a house, renting a room. Yet, this place had two bedrooms, ground floor and first floor house. We did not have to share a room with other strangers. The house in Park street had no paper bills; we just had to top-up the electronic meter every week and top-up the oil tank to heat the boiler. The rent cost was reduced when we moved in and we did not have to spend a significant amount of money on the furniture or kitchen appliances.

The Town was just round the corner from the house and therefore we did not have to travel too far to evangelise. The Train and Bus Stations was five minutes' walk away. This was a dream house we had always prayed for. Moreover, the place was so easy to find that people could visit at any time to have fellowship.

Unforgettable Year

We had the opportunity to use this house for house group fellowships, Bible studies and prayer meetings. We also provided lunch and dinner to 154 believers and non-believers. Sarah had regular income from the University of Ulster and David and Hannah had a great response from the public at the Coleraine Town Centre during the open-air mission. Our Ministry was prospering and many people had interest in our Ministry work for the first time.

Cottage for You - Limerick in Republic of Ireland

We tried various methods (such as car and caravan, buses, trains, ferry, coach holidays) to evangelise in different Town Centres across the United Kingdom, yet cottage holiday was a new method which we did not pursue. It was our first time of hearing of such holiday packages, which was quite unusual for the Choi Family.

1000 Years As One Day

Apparently, there were over 18,000 personally inspected holiday cottages which you could choose from across the UK and Ireland. This meant that Sarah had to apply through the online system, select the duration of stay (usually there is a limit as to how many days you can book) and pay in advance, then on the day of arrival at the cottage, the owner gives you the key and you can rent out a property for one week, in any location. We had always suffered and felt uncomfortable staying with other people within their house. Therefore, by booking the holiday cottage, we could go out and share the Gospel and come back knowing that we had a roof over our head, sleep comfortably, being able to cook homemade meals, and being ready for tomorrow's mission outreach. The only slight problem we encountered was that these holiday cottages were located in rural areas, and we had a great problem with regard to transportation from the cottage to the nearest Town Centre.

Unforgettable Year

It would have been an ideal holiday package if David was still able to drive but because of the fact that we had no car meant that we were reliant on the public transportation system. Especially in the Republic of Ireland, the transportation was not reliable at all.

On this occasion we had Robert and Ann helping us with the transport from Belfast to Limerick, which was 200miles (322km) and five hours journey by car. We had known Robert and Ann in Northern Ireland, who always supplied us with Gospel tracts and cared for our family in so many ways. During our car journey, Ann bought us three breakfasts and tea, equipping us for this mission journey to the Republic of Ireland. When we arrived at the cottage in Ashford, Limerick, South Ireland, on Saturday, we were 28miles (45km) away from the Town Centre.

1000 Years As One Day

There were no shops nearby and no transportations. Sarah should have asked the Cottage for You agent as to whether there were transportations and shops nearby but because of her first experience we were placed in a rural location. As David walked out of the cottage and as he looked around, there was one large Catholic Church.

David wrote down the telephone number of the Catholic Priest and asked Sarah to give the Priest a call. David said, *"We ought to sing at this Catholic Church on Sunday and then when people greet us, let's inform them of our situation. The Lord will help us."* With huge faith Sarah contacted the Priest and requested to sing during the mass service. Thankfully the Priest gave us the permission to sing *'How Great Thou Art'* on Sunday morning during the mass service.

Unforgettable Year

On Sunday, towards the end of the mass service, the Catholic members thanked us for the contribution at the mass service. They welcomed, greeted and asked us a few questions with regard to where we were staying and how long for. We told them that we were staying at the holiday cottage around the corner and were here on a mission trip. Then one lady, called Caroline, in particular, who had taken a great interest, asked us a few more questions. Then she said the following, *"I live only a few roads down from where you are. Could I come and visit you late afternoon and we can have a chat about your mission work."* When Caroline visited the cottage we were staying in, we had great fellowship and she said she would help us with transportation, since she worked in a Limerick hospital. We all agreed to meet outside the cottage at 7.30am the following day and Caroline would come and pick us up and drop us off outside the hospital, where there was a bus stop which was a short ride to the Town Centre.

In the late afternoon, we would meet Caroline again at the hospital and she would take us back to our cottage in Ashford. During the time we were driving, Sarah shared her testimony about the Lord and had a great conversation with Caroline (she was a very religious Catholic). When Sarah had conversation with Caroline, she questioned about the Bible and how little she knew about the Gospel. Caroline did not know that Jesus was resurrected from the dead and the way of Salvation is through the blood of Jesus Christ. She had always believed that being good mattered and praying to Rachel was crucial, and confessing her sins to the Catholic Priest was absolutely important. Yet, Caroline never thought about being *'saved'* or being *'Born again.'* Certainly the conversation made her think. On the last day of that week, as we were travelling back to the cottage, Caroline asked about Heaven. She then confessed the following, *"I know that I am a sinner and the only assurance of Heaven is through the blood of Jesus Christ."*

Unforgettable Year

Caroline accepted the Lord as her Saviour. After sharing the Gospel with Caroline, She had the confidence to say that she has become a child of God.

Mission Journey by Airplanes

We always thought that without a passport, travelling by air was not permitted. Since David and Sarah had lost their passports while clearing the house in Preston, Lancashire, we had always taken the longer route to travel between Northern Ireland and England. One day, Sarah researched into a more comfortable way to travel a long distance. Travelling by the Cross Channel Bus Service was extremely exhausting and time consuming. When Sarah investigated the website, she found out that there were planes which was low-cost carriers and operated on a short flight services. This meant that the travelling journey between Belfast International to London only lasted one hour.

Due to the low-cost of the ticket the airplanes provided a limited service, nevertheless it was an effective way to travel between Northern Ireland and England. Sarah enquired to *'Ryanair Airlines'* with regard to the identification card, and the booking procedures. They confirmed that UK provisional licences were acceptable to use for identification when travelling in the United Kingdom. There was no need for passports. The bookings were carried out online and once the payment had been accepted, the confirmation email comes through with a barcode which you have to display at the baggage area, through the security and when boarding. We had already been on the long flight from London Heathrow to Inchon, South Korea. The flight lasted over 11 hours. We enjoyed being on the airplanes and this was a precious expensive method to travel.

Unforgettable Year

With regard to the low-cost carrier airplanes, they had strict policy about the luggage allowances; because of small cabin size. Each passenger is allowed one piece of hand baggage on board and with regard to musical instruments, extra seat must be booked or £50 paid in order to use this service. For our amplifier, we had to pay additional fee (as a large luggage of 15 kg). Every time we used the airplane service, we had to go through the rigorous security checks which were no different to being on board a flight which lasts much longer. We had used three airlines (Ryanair, easyJet and Flybe). We did not approve of the service of Ryanair but we had better welcomes from easyJet and Flybe.

We used the short flight services every month from November 2015 to June 2016, visiting 39 Town Centres in Highlands, Jersey (Channel Island) Bedfordshire, Kent, Somerset, Lancashire, Bristol and Bath.

We had been on 16 aircrafts flying from Northern Ireland to England in order to share the Gospel. We spent £5,626.91 to reach the above mentioned areas. The cost also included travelling on the aircrafts, buses, trains, taxis and accommodations. The total cost excluded our food costs. It was amazing how the Lord provided for us and blessed us with the finances to cover these areas in England.

Alex - Online Video Ministry

When we were living in Park street, Coleraine, Northern Ireland, we had been devotedly sharing the Gospel in Coleraine Town Centre. Since we were carrying out the Singing Ministry on a daily basis, people started to take an interest in our Ministry. One day, David and Hannah met a gentleman called Alex. He was originally born in Honduras and worked in Belize.

Unforgettable Year

When we met Alex, he had a filming studio in Coleraine. He had specialised in producing 60 second videos for companies. As he saw David and Hannah's Singing Ministry, he was greatly touched by the Ministry and asked whether the Choi Family would be interested in being filmed. He proposed a live filming during the outreach in Coleraine, in order to produce a 60 second video about our Ministry. This would be published on YouTube online channel and the website link could be used in various third party websites and on Facebook pages. It was a great way to let other people know about the Choi Family Ministry.

We met a few weeks later. He had brought his video production team, shooting camera and various pieces of equipment for filming. This brought a lot of attention to the public passing through Coleraine Town Centre.

The first video was extremely successful and once the video shooting was accomplished, we visited Alex's filming studio and prayed for his business. He carefully edited the video and we made our first short video of the Choi Family Ministry. Alex did not charge us for his hard work, since his father was also a Church Minister and this was a contribution towards the work of God. We were grateful to the Lord for Alex and his talent in serving the Lord.

Once the first video was published on YouTube, Alex offered to produce a 60 second video clip of David's preaching. Therefore, every evening time between 4-5pm and 6-7pm, we had to prepare the sermon script and send it to Alex via email in advance. David and Sarah visited the filming studio to record David's preaching. We prepared seven sermon scripts and Alex filmed seven videos of David's preaching.

This was then uploaded on to the YouTube website. Alex was informing us that the preaching message was being well received by countries like Philippines, Belize and India. Alex also contacted us before Christmas time, asking us to attend his filming studio, since he wanted to film a Christmas message from the Choi Family. The video which was uploaded on YouTube channel entitled, *'Season's Greetings from the Choi Family.'* In total Alex produced nine videos for the Choi Family Ministry. This was a new opening of the online video Ministry; touching people's lives through the online media channels.

William - Keep on Singing

During our mission work in Coleraine, there was an Irish man who had silver shoulder length hair, wearing a long coat, and always walked pass us with his two arms open like a human airplane.

He would always shout out, *"Keep singing, Keep singing."* He had never approached us before to have further conversation. We did not know who he was but we knew that he was a little indifferent but really enjoyed our Singing Ministry. Then, we began to get to know this man, as he was called William and was a dedicated Christian and a member of St. Patricks Church. One day William asked David a question, *"Have you ever been to a concert to sing?"* David did not reply to this unexpected question. William said that he was involved in a Radio Ministry and that he was planning to do a concert in August time.

William said that there were other famous Gospel music singers in Northern Ireland taking part in the concert and he asked us to take part and sing six songs in total. The Gospel concert schedule was divided into a first half and second half.

Unforgettable Year

William wanted us to sing three pieces in the first half and then another three pieces in the second half of the concert. We were delighted with this opportunity. This concert was advertised in the local newspaper.

The stage was beautiful and there were approximately 12 seats on the stage. All the Gospel artists were required to take a seat at this place. At that evening we had over 300 people attending the concert. It was a huge success and people cheered as each songs finished. When we sang our last piece, *'Pass Me Not O gentle Saviour'*; some of the Gospel artists which were on the stage wept. This concert was filmed and the DVD was presented to us, free of charge. We also had a donation from William towards our Singing Ministry. Later that year, William invited us back again to his concert which was held in Portrush town hall, in October 8pm.

Due to the weather, the number of attendees was not as many as the one in August but still was a great opportunity to let people know about our Ministry.

George - Radio Ministry

After three years of serving the Lord in Coleraine, Northern Ireland, we started to receive a significant amount of opposition from the shop keepers. The general public (who were anti-Christ) started to make complaints and a few police officers visited us at Park street during the winter times. One afternoon, we had unexpected visitor standing outside our house. A well-built gentleman in his 50s, he looked rather tough and we assumed that it was another public member arriving at our door step to make a complaint. David put the chain on the door and opened the front door gate, leaving enough space to speak but preventing the person from entering the house.

Unforgettable Year

The gentleman said, *"Look, can I come inside and speak to you?"* David opened the door and was not pleased by his request. The gentleman said, *"Ok, here is my card. My name is George and I am the owner of the Radio North."* David then looked at George and then invited him into the living room. David then called Sarah, since she was working from home upstairs. Sarah was not expecting visitors; and was not really pleased with the fact that she had to come downstairs. George then looked around and said, *"Who speaks English?"* Sarah said, *"Go ahead, what is the enquiry?"* George laughed out loud and said, *"Oh great, thank goodness you speak some English. Look Sarah, I was watching your mum and dad singing in the Coleraine Town Centre and people has been telling me some positive things about your Singing Ministry. They just love you and the singing. I was hoping to have you guys broadcasting on my radio station. Well, not my station but it is the Lords. I want to give you 15 to 30 minutes slot for you to do a programme for me."*

1000 Years As One Day

We had never broadcast on the radio before, and we did not have a clue as to how we were supposed to plan a programme for 15 to 30 minutes. George said, *"Have you got any songs recorded?"* Sarah replied, *"No songs recorded and we have no experience of radio broadcasting. How is it done George?"* He laughed and said, *"Don't you worry Sarah! We will get you sorted." George* had given us half an hour to broadcast on Radio North for free of charge. This was the best present we could ask for.

George had a contact called Tom, who specialised in recording, editing and producing CDs and DVDs. He had a studio with relevant equipment for recording professional music. His wife and daughter were also well-known composers and song-writers. Tom controlled most of the Radio North programmes and had been helping George with regard to the radio station work for over 20 years.

Unforgettable Year

At our first meeting with Tom at his home studio, we had brought a guitar, music stand and some music sheets. Sarah had brought a script for the voice recording (such as introducing the Choi Family Radio Ministry, some personal testimonies). Since Sarah had never broadcast on a radio before, she was hoping that Tom would contribute with the voice recording. Tom also had his own radio programme and said that the audience does not want to hear the same voice over and over again. Tom encouraged Sarah to take up this opportunity and be the presenter for the Choi Family Radio Ministry. Sarah was extremely nervous but according to Tom, Sarah's voice appeared to be natural and not offensive to listeners. We then worked on the song recordings. Tom had a great Roland piano, which Sarah played to accompany David and Hannah's singing.

Then Tom had brought two sets of professional microphones in order to record David and Hannah's voice separately. Piano recording was separate and David and Hannah's voices were separate. The only musical item we could not separate to record was the guitar, since David can only sing naturally while strumming his guitar. This meant that David had to strum the guitar very gently so that the sound does not get mixed up with his voice recording. It was a real challenge for the Choi Family. We were not experts and it was difficult to make a masterpiece.

However, with God's grace, we were able to record 11 songs to be broadcasted live on Radio North. Tom's hard work was immense and yet he never charged us a penny for his work. We thank God for his dedication and contribution towards the Choi Family Ministry.

Unforgettable Year

The songs that were recorded sounded superb and we were very delighted with the master copy. Tom and Sarah had put together a programme and sent it to George for approval. Then George asked Tom, *"Who played the piano? It sounded beautiful!"* Tom said that it was Sarah. George did not know that Sarah played the piano but when he heard the programme he was extremely happy. Then, George insisted Tom to start the broadcasting from the first Sunday of the following month.

Once the broadcasting cycle started, Tom and Sarah had to put together a schedule every week. It was intense and a significant amount of time was dedicated towards the Radio Ministry. Sarah never presented on a radio before, nor did she learn how to play the piano professionally. Also David and Hannah never made an official CD before nor were they qualified singers but the Lord used the Choi Family in a mighty way.

George called every week to encourage the Choi Family. George heard and received much positive feedback from listeners, that they were enjoying the programmes. Apparently one gentleman, who walked away from the Church, came back to Church after hearing one of our radio programmes. The Lord was touching people's lives through the Choi Family Radio Ministry.

Monica - European Family

Monica and her three sons called Adam, Chris and Daniel were living in Coleraine, County Londonderry. She was married to an Irish man called Peter; however the marriage did not last because of Peter committing a criminal offence. Our family known Peter from the time we lived in the Circular Road and we met his parents.

Unforgettable Year

Our family shared the Gospel with Peter and his parents and certainly Peter enjoyed our Singing Ministry and asked David to pray for him on many occasions. We knew of Peter's criminal offence and he was not righteous before God. Therefore, we continually counselled him and prayed for him. Then on a following year, we met Monica and her three children. They had been very touched by our Ministry and wanted to have further fellowship with our family.

When Monica explained her marriage situation and further described her ex-husband, it matched Peter's family and lifestyle. Sarah said, *"Monica, what is the name of your husband?"* Monica replied, *"His name is Peter."* Then there was a silence. Monica was surprised that we knew her ex-husband. Due to Peter's criminal offence, he could not see his children. The three boys, Adam, Chris and Daniel had never spent time with their father.

1000 Years As One Day

It was really a heart-breaking situation, especially, Adam had been diagnosed with autism, and Monica found it extremely hard to take care of three boys as a single mum. However, Monica loved the Lord; despite her circumstances she continued to share the Gospel with other people on a one-to-one basis. She had become fond of our family and regularly had long conversations about the Christian life and the *'Religious Churches in Coleraine Town Centre.'* With Monica's family and the Choi family, we had initially started to plant a Church in Milburn Community Centre and later at the University Chaplin. Hannah had received the minister's ordination from South Korea, so it was her duty and call to preach at the services. Sarah led the service in English and then Hannah preached in Korean. Sarah then translated Hannah's preaching in to English, while focusing the teaching towards the three boys. Monica led the prayer time and gave personal testimonies.

Unforgettable Year

Sometimes we had the boys reading the Bible, encouraging them to be strong in the Word of God. Monica always desired her boys to be strong in the Word of God and very much appreciated Sarah for her time and dedication in teaching her children about the Bible. When our family had begun to know Monica's family, we had realised that they never travelled to other parts of Ireland or England. They always lived in Coleraine Town Centre. Sarah felt that it was important for the boys to explore other parts of the country, and this would be a great opportunity for them to enhance their learning. Therefore, Sarah suggested to Monica the following; *"During the Easter break, we are thinking of travelling to Enniskillen to share the Gospel. We wondered if you and the boys could come with us? We will book a bed and breakfast nearby and explore various parts of Enniskillen, do some fun activities for the boys after the outreach at the Town Centre?"* This was exciting news for the three boys and Monica.

1000 Years As One Day

They never ventured from Coleraine and it was their first time visiting Enniskillen. Once we had confirmation from Monica's family, Sarah researched into various suitable places to stay. Then there was a place called, *"The farm house at Hilary's bed and breakfast."* This place was not far away from Enniskillen Town Centre and it was located in the heart of Fermanagh. This place had animals (such as cows and rabbits) which was quite interesting for the young boys.

Moreover, near the farm house, there was Florence court house (trees, gardens and fun activities) as well as the Marble Arch Caves Geo Park, where there were children activities. Marble Arch Caves had a series of natural limestone under the cave which was an interesting event for children and great opportunity for learning. We booked three nights with Hilary and seven of us travelled to Enniskillen to take up these activities mentioned above.

Unforgettable Year

The boys really enjoyed the activities in Enniskillen. On the last day we had taken the boys swimming. When we arrived at the swimming pool, the boys were frightened of the changing room. They needed a *'father figure'* to be with them. Since they did not have a father, David went inside the changing room and helped the boys to get changed. Then Monica and the Choi family went and sat in the spectators' area to watch the boys playing in the swimming pool. After this activity we had gone to the restaurant and had ice cream.

For Monica and her family, it was the best event they have done in their lives. Monica was so grateful to the Choi Family. She thanked us in return by helping our Ministry financially with food and clothes, supporting us with the Church planting and outreach programmes. Due to Monica's devotion and support with regard to Church planting, Hannah had the opportunity to deliver 42 sermons and we had 20 people attending the services in Coleraine.

We had a mixture of people around the world such as the Korean couple, European family, Chinese family, Irish, Welsh and English couple, family from Belize attending our services. It was ten months of ministering the Word of God to a group of families from around the world. Our Church planting in London was not so successful but we were grateful to the Lord for this short but successful Church planting activity.

Chapter 21

Moving to Belfast

Notice to Move

After serving the Lord devotedly in Coleraine Town Centre for the last four years, we had a notice from the estate agent to move out of Park street, Coleraine, Northern Ireland. We predicted that this would happen since the opposition from the shop keepers in Coleraine had increased. In addition a few of the members who had been causing a significant amount of opposition knew where we were residing, which impacted on the property we lived in.

1000 Years As One Day

However, when we received a letter from the estate agent asking us to leave, we knew that the work we had accomplished in Coleraine had come to an end and this was a calling from God to move on and depart from this Town Centre. While living in Coleraine Town, we had been very fruitful within our Ministry and it was time for us to move to a new location. David had always wanted to move to the centre of Northern Ireland, in Belfast, since, there was more opportunity to travel beyond Northern Ireland and to move to England. He had also thought that there would be more openings for the Choi Family Ministry. Therefore, in order to find suitable accommodation in Belfast, our family caught the train on 7th August to Belfast City Centre. Then when we arrived there, we walked 7miles (11km) around Belfast City Centre, looking for private or small estate agents. Sarah attempted to search online but this investigation of properties was not very successful.

Moving to Belfast

We had always accomplished house searches using a traditional method, by visiting the estate agent in person. This was a more effective way to book house viewings and then to sort out paper work.

Trevor - English Gentleman

The day was darkening and we had not met any helpful people at the estate agents. Then, while walking through Belfast City Centre, without having much food, drink or rest, there was a sudden rain and wind. So we opened up our umbrella, but the wind had been so severe that the umbrella had turned inside out and broke the edge of the fibreglass shaft and ribs. We could not hold on to the flimsy fabric and it was no use. Therefore, we decided to put the two umbrellas in the bin. Then, within five minutes of walking without an umbrella, we were soaked through to the skin.

1000 Years As One Day

Hannah and Sarah tried to persuade David to go back home, while David kept on walking forward. Hannah and Sarah were extremely frustrated and yet, David turned right into the Elim Church. We walked inside being soaked and wet. We walked into a service and some gentleman was preaching.

However, there was this cold atmosphere, people had seen us being soaked by the rain, yet no one seemed to approach us, or even care about these foreigners entering into the Church. Even after the service, we sat for a while but no one seemed to greet us. Then one well-built English guy, in his late 50s, wearing old rugged clothes came up to us and started the conversation. This gentleman was called Trevor; he was a care taker of the Elim Church. He said, *"Is everything alright? Did you want something to eat or drink?"* David had mentioned about our accommodation circumstances and requested help.

Moving to Belfast

Trevor offered to give up his accommodation for that evening and gave us his room to sleep in for that night. His room was covered with Bibles and Christian books; there was a double bed and a small en-suite bathroom within the room. The room was not tidy and we barely slept for that evening.

However, Trevor had been very kind to us giving three strangers the key for that room and did not charge us for that night. Since we did not have any spare clothes, he gave us few clothes and socks to change for that evening. Trevor then came back to his flat the following day and helped us with transport, working as a mediator to speak to the local estate agents. However, it was unfortunate that we could not find any accommodation in Belfast within those last two days.

Therefore, we went to the place where Trevor worked. He worked in a Charity shop owned by Pastors from a local Nigerian Church in Belfast. He was the delivery driver for that Charity shop. They had a large van to deliver goods or to receive goods. Since we had no success from house hunting, we thanked Trevor for his generosity and kindness, handed back the room key and informed Trevor that we were going to head back to Coleraine.

Trevor then said, *"If you need to comeback at any time, I could let you have that room again. Also if you are struggling to find a more permanent place to live in Belfast, I could move out of that room and leave my stuff down stairs and then you guys could have my room."* We thanked Trevor for his offer but we could not see our family moving into Trevor's flat permanently. Since there were other men living in that flat and using the same kitchen. The place was extremely untidy and unhygienic.

Moving to Belfast

Last Day at Park Street

When we arrived at the house in Park street, we realised how much the Lord had been blessing us. The last two days were toilsome and we were so glad to be *'Home'* again. The days were passing by and after five days of hunting house around the Coleraine and Belfast areas, the Choi Family decided to move into Trevor's house temporarily and then search for a better home while living in Trevor's flat. Therefore, Sarah called Trevor on the phone and requested to move into Trevor's property at the end of the month. Trevor agreed to that decision and he helped us with the house move.

Our Park street neighbour Karen was extremely sad to see us leave Coleraine. Also a former Mayer of Coleraine, George and few others we had known in Coleraine was extremely upset because of our move. On our last day, George and Karen gave us a hug and said, *"Keep in touch!"*

When we look back within the last few years in Coleraine, we had devoutly sowed the seed of the Gospel. We had seen people healed from sicknesses and an alcoholic man repenting and turning back to Jesus. According to a group of people, because of our Singing Ministry, they had the privilege of leading 300 people to Jesus. It was time that the Lord moved us on to the new area to expand our Singing Ministry.

Finding New Opportunities

After four days of hunting for the house, we agreed to move into Lagan View Court in Belfast. We could not move in to the apartment straight away and had to wait two additional weeks and three days. Therefore, we continuously stayed at the Trevor's property. The room we had at Trevor's was not comfortable for us, since the room was extremely small. Nevertheless, we thanked the Lord and continued to serve the Lord.

Moving to Belfast

While at this place we had evangelised in Lisburn Town Centre every Saturday. In addition, Trevor invited us to his Bible study at the Nigerian Church, between 6.30-9pm. We were encouraged to sing for an hour every Wednesday to a group of people attending the Church. He gave us a little financial support for our Ministry, which was a great help.

On Sundays, we had been visiting various Churches in Belfast, in order to let other people know about our Ministry. We were also looking for a building where we could start a *'Community Centre'*, feeding the homeless, teaching people English and computer skills etc. However, the Pastors of the Church in Belfast undermined our capabilities and just wanted to see us attending their Church service.

We had the zeal for Jesus and the *'Religious Pastors'* saw us as being a member of their Church, just filling in the Church seats, paying regular tithes. Ministers at these Christian Churches were not interested in the work we were doing for the Lord. Nor were they inclined to give us any prayer or financial support. We were extremely upset and frustrated by these *'Religious Churches.'* Despite this depressing situation, our family continued to serve the Lord Jesus, following His footsteps.

Gerald - North Belfast

One Saturday late evening, Sarah had been searching Churches online. Then, we came across a small Church based in North Belfast. Sarah had rang the Pastor in charge and asked if we could visit the Church the following morning and have some fellowship. At that time, Pastor Gerald answered the phone and was delighted to hear from us.

Moving to Belfast

Gerald's Church had been suffering for a while, as many members had passed away because of their age and the numbers of the congregation decreased. Gerald was placed in a rough estate area to Pastor a Church. Gerald was suffering from burnout, because of exhaustion, since the head of the Church had not given him much support or resources.

There were approximately 15 people attending the Church, who were quite elderly. There was no one to help him to open the Church, to maintain the Church building or to give a hand with transporting members to their homes. When we arrived in the morning, we had the opportunity to lead worship music. Gerald was so pleased to have some live music at the Church. The congregation enjoyed the worship and gave Gerald positive feedback. One member said, *"Can we keep them, Gerald? They are so lovely. You are coming back next week, aren't you?"* an elderly lady's request was so sincere.

How could we say no! Gerald suggested meeting us the following day to invite us for a lunch at a business place where he used to work. We gladly accepted his invitation. Gerald had been informing us of the Church situation and that he needed help. Therefore, we did help him with providing the worship service for a few weeks on Sundays. On the day when we moved to Lagan view court, he had been very helpful in transporting our household items from Trevor's flat to the new apartment. He helped us on a few occasions with the finances for our Ministry as well.

Moving to Lagan View Court

While living in Lagan view court, we had been so blessed to find this spectacular apartment, overseeing the Lagan River, Hilton hotel and the Waterfront Hall. The scenery from our balcony was so beautiful.

Moving to Belfast

The monthly rent was twice as much as the Park street but the property we moved into was a better location for us to travel from Belfast to London. Our family felt that the Lord was giving us an award after four years of Singing Ministry in Coleraine and suffering in silence at Trevor's accommodation. We were grateful to the Lord for His care, love and mercy. Our family continued with our Singing Ministry every Saturday in Lisburn and attended Trevor's Bible study on Wednesday evenings.

The time passed, when we lived in Lagan view court for three months. Then, in November 2016, our family opened the map to see areas where we did not visit before. We realised that there were approximately 10 Town Centres we had not visited around the South of England. We needed funding to reach those areas. We prayed about this situation and contacted our supporter Pastor Donald. We shared our prayers and vision.

1000 Years As One Day

Pastor Donald did not question us any further and sent us donations to cover the cost for transport and accommodation. Our family then booked a flight from Belfast International to London Gatwick, which was 495miles (797km), and then when we arrived at Gatwick airport, caught the train to Bournemouth (115miles/ 185km). From Bournemouth Travel Lodge, we travelled to Poole and Dorchester to share the Gospel. Then we moved our accommodation to Poole, and then travelled to Yeovil and Aldershot. We moved our hotel locations several times to reach various areas in the South of England. In total we travelled over 1,767miles (2,844km) and visited 13 Town Centres to preach the Word of God. The total costs of our travel and accommodation came to £1,366.50. We spent a little over our funding, but we had the opportunity to share about our Ministry work in Crawley Redeemed Church of God, who then collected a love offering towards our mission work.

Moving to Belfast

God had been faithful and His compassion did not fail. He provided us with our every need during that London mission trip.

December 2016 in Belfast

When we arrived at the Lagan view court, Trevor suggested that the Pastor Immanuel from the Nigerian Church wanted to invite us to their Church carol service on 18th December. Pastor Immanuel wanted us to be part of their carol service and to minister in songs. We gladly accepted his invitation and had a great opportunity to take part in a successful carol service. Following from this day, we had another call from Trevor. He was involved with the night shelter work for the Nigerian Church, and he wanted to see if we would come on 24th evening at 9pm and help with delivering food to the homeless and meet some of the Romanians.

1000 Years As One Day

Our family had never been invited to this type of mission work before, so we gladly accepted this opportunity. On 24th December 2016, Trevor and our family met at 9pm and we started to look around Belfast City Centre to find homeless people. After walking around over 20,000 steps around the City Centre, we found six homeless people. We approached them and handed out sandwiches and water. Then, we had the opportunity to talk about the importance of the birth of Jesus, and the real meaning of Christmas.

The homeless people in Belfast were well looked after, they had a lot of food and blankets to keep them warm. We offered them accommodation to sleep inside a warm building, yet they refused to take up this option. Since, they were so comfortable in the way they lived; these homeless people did not seem to desire anything. One thing we learnt from this experience is that people from Belfast loved to take care of the homeless people and we felt reassured.

Moving to Belfast

As soon as we could not find any more homeless people, we made our way to two Romanian houses. Sarah searched online to find Psalm 23 in Romanian and she had carefully hand written this scripture for the family. They were so delighted to see the Bible scripture in their own language. According to one family member, Sarah had good Romanian writing skills. Sarah shared the importance of reading the Bible and then asked one of the members to read out loud in Romanian Psalm 23. We had a time of prayer and Trevor gave a box of fundamental basic food items for the two families.

Christmas Day 2016

David had a great desire to move back to London. Sarah and Hannah could not see how we could move back to such an expensive area to continue our mission work. Despite opposition from Hannah and Sarah, David kept on praying for open doors in London.

1000 Years As One Day

The Lord was laying on our heart to move away from Northern Ireland and return back to London in England. More work needed to be accomplished in London in comparison with places in Belfast, Northern Ireland. Then on Christmas day we had a gentleman in his late 70s call us. He originated from Sri Lanka and lived in Croydon, London. He wished us well for the New Year and gave us Christmas greetings. We met this gentleman during our outreach in Croydon a month ago. When we met him, he was not well and asked us to pray for him. The day when he called us, we asked him about his health. He said that it was much better and thanked us for the prayers. He wanted to contribute towards our Ministry every month and requested our bank details. Sarah mentioned the following to the gentleman, *"Sir, we feel that the Lord is asking us to move back to London and continue serving the Lord there. Do you know anyone who could provide accommodation?"*

Moving to Belfast

The gentleman said, *"I don't know but I can ask a few people and let you know."* A week had gone by and then the gentleman called us. He said that his daughter lived in West Wickham in Kent, and the gentleman said, *"Can you speak to my daughter?"* The daughter was on the phone to Sarah. She said, *"My father had told me about your mission work and we would like to help you."* She was a Chartered Accountant in Central London and her husband was a Manager at a local supermarket. They had a spacious house and offered us a place to stay. It was just amazing, how the Lord was opening doors. They did not charge us for the stay and gave us a spacious room which included an en-suite bathroom. The only thing the Sri Lankan family requested was to help with the house chores and to assist them with looking after their nine year old daughter. We agreed to this and started to pack our household items in Belfast, Lagan view court.

Richard - Transporting Items to London

Our family was determined to pack all our household items and depart Lagan view court at the end of the year 2016. Therefore, we urgently needed to find a friend to help us with moving the items from Belfast to London. We initially asked Trevor, if he knew any way of moving our household items back to London. He suggested that a cargo with a pallet would fit all the household items, which could be transported from Belfast to London. The cost seemed to be reasonably cheap. However, we did not feel reassured.

We wanted to find a friend who could load our items and travel with us from Belfast to London by a van or a large vehicle with a trailer. One evening, while our family was walking around Belfast Town Centre, Sarah suggested that we ought to call Richard. We met him at Paul and Ann's Prayer Union Meeting.

Moving to Belfast

Richard previously provided accommodation for us and had helped us with transport in the past. He used to work as a part-time taxi driver. He enjoyed driving and this might be something he could be interested in. Hence, Sarah gave Richard a call. When he answered the phone, his voice was extremely weak (which was very unusual). Richard explained that he damaged his ribs, falling off his car. Sarah could not understand how he could damage his ribs, falling off a standard Passat Volkswagen vehicle. Richard said that he changed his vehicle to a 4x4 Jeep open back. After his explanation, Sarah could understand the reason for his damage. Richard asked the reason for the call. Sarah explained that our family was planning to move to London and needed some help with transporting our belongings. Then without Richard giving it much thought, he bluntly said, *"I will do it!"* Sarah thought this would be impossible for him to take up this difficult task, especially with his rib injury.

1000 Years As One Day

Richard was determined that he could do this, since he could not lie down to sleep in the evening because of pain and he would rather sit upright and drive through the night. We then made an agreement to meet Richard at Belfast train station the following day to invite him to Lagan view court. Richard needed to examine the quantity of our household belongings to estimate whether these items would fit inside his vehicle. When Richard arrived at our property, he said that we would need an additional trailer to fit all our household items.

Our family did not know who would have a trailer for hire. Richard was confident that a friend of his had a spacious trailer which would sort out the problem. Sarah then booked the ferry online for four passengers, one vehicle and one trailer from Belfast to Stranraer, departing at 6am.

Moving to Belfast

The last day of December 2016, we agreed to meet at 12.30am to load all the household items. Richard joined us at this time but he had forgotten to bring the waterproof cover for the trailer, so he drove back to his home and joined us again by 1.30am and then we departed to the ferry port. We arrived too early, so we waited inside the vehicle until we had further instruction from the ferry team. Our family agreed to pay for Richard's vehicle's fuel costs, food and drinks and ferry cost. Due to his large vehicle, the fuel cost was more than what we had expected.

In total it had cost us £704.50 to move our items from Belfast to West Wickham. The journey from Belfast to West Wickham was over 471miles (758km) and we travelled by car for over 14 hours to reach the Sri Lankan family's house. We were all exhausted and frustrated. During that journey, Richard was waiting to hear from the Doctor with regard to his ribs.

He thought that the ribs were broken, but the Doctor confirmed that the ribs were not broken and it was the muscle strains which caused the pain. Richard felt that the Lord healed him during the time he had been working for the Lord, delivering the Choi Family goods to London.

Chapter 22

Final Call - Back to London

London Road

We had initially moved to West Wickham and then because of the Sri Lankan's personal and family circumstances, we were asked to move out on the 2nd February 2017. This meant that it was our fourth time of moving house within the space of six months. We have never moved houses this frequently before. It was a really hard time at the start of 2017. After this suffering had passed, the Lord blessed us with a secured flat in London Road, West Croydon at the end of March 2017.

1000 Years As One Day

This flat was very basic but suited us perfectly, since West Croydon station is only a five minute walk away, with great 24 hour transport service. The cost of our rent is triple the rent in Northern Ireland, yet the Lord had not once let us suffer by not meeting the rent payments. The Lord directed us to this place for a reason. We believe that there is always a time, season and reason for everything when doing the work of the Lord. In fact, London Road is a well-known place for dealing drugs. There are a significant amount of alcoholics surrounding this street.

Christian supporters have been worried and extremely surprised to see us living in the roughest and most dangerous area. Yet, the Lord kept us in a safe flat where there are three levels of security systems. We felt extremely peaceful when we made a contract for this flat.

Final Call - Back to London

It had been two months of living in this place and already we befriended local alcoholics and they have regularly attended our Sunday open-air meetings in Croydon. Indeed, London Road may not be the place we might stay for a long-term basis. Yet, for the time being until the Lord moves us on to another place, we are doing our very best to pray for this street and asking the Lord to perform miracles. We are praying that the Lord will reduce the number of alcoholics and drug addicts and for the police officers to quickly recognise the criminals in this street. We have already seen some changes: police officers are less frequently visiting London Road and evenings are beginning to be quieter than few months ago.

London Mission Work Continues

It has been ten years that we have been travelling around other parts of Great Britain and Ireland. This meant that our family still had a few places around the Boroughs of London we had not evangelised before. Therefore, we asked the Lord for boldness and strength to travel to Town Centres around London to share the Gospel of Jesus Christ. In the year of 2017, we travelled over 2,760miles (4,442km) visiting 24 Town Centres.

We have travelled to nine new Town Centres which include: Gravesend, Lewes, Andover, Newbury, Luton, Greenwich, Chatham, Dartford and Gillingham. Then the Lord led us to focus on five Town Centres near Croydon such as: Sutton, Mitcham, Lewisham, Redhill and Kingston.

Final Call - Back to London

We are working on building relationships with the communities within these targeted Town Centres. Pastoring the homeless, drug addicts and alcoholics; visiting homes and having good fellowship with those who are lonely, neglected and widowed, leading people to Jesus in a more personal way and taking care of those that are less able.

Amanda - Sutton in South London

There had been quite a significant amount of rejection to the Gospel in Sutton. Due to this rejection of the Gospel, Sarah encountered various reactions (such as swearing, cursing and shouting). We reported this to some of the local Churches and asked them to join with us in prayer for Sutton Town Centre. Then one morning, as we were sharing the Gospel, worshiping the Lord in the open-air, we had an English lady in her early 40s, standing behind David and Hannah and trying to sing along with the hymn, *"I have found a friend in Jesus."*

Sarah quickly came behind the lady and guided her along the words of the songs. This lady was called Amanda. She was singing and doing all the actions as she was singing the words *"He (Jesus) is everything to me."* Then the song continued with, *"In sorrow He is my comfort, in trouble He is my stay…"* These words must have greatly touched her. Sarah approached Amanda and said, *"You sing very well!"* Then suddenly, Amanda put her both hands on her face and said, *"Oh, I need help, I really need help."* She started to walk away and cried. Sarah held tightly on to Amanda's hand and tried to reassure her and said, *"What is the matter, please tell me."* Then Amanda said, *"I have a bag of medications in my bag and I was going to kill myself today, because I hate myself and I don't want to live anymore, I have been brutally abused… I hate myself."* Amanda was going to take an overdose of medication. Sarah opened both arms wide and hugged the lady and said, *"Please don't take your life.*

Final Call - Back to London

Your life is too precious in the eyes of God. Jesus loves you so much, come back to Him and He will take care of you." Amanda said, *"I need Jesus in my life, yes I need Jesus in my life."* Sarah and Amanda sat down on a bench outside the shopping centre in order to have a deeper conversation. Then Amanda explained the following of what had happened during her childhood. She witnessed her mother shooting herself with a gun (suicidal) at the age of thirteen. This impacted on her mental health. Since then, she had been mixing with a group of the wrong people, learning to take drugs and alcohol. She had been associating with wrong relationships, where these men had abused her, which made her feel disgusted and worthless.

Amanda had shown a scar on both her arms where she had been harming herself. Amanda had used a broken glass bottle to cut her arteries.

She had another broken glass in her pocket, which she took out and showed to Sarah. As soon as she had shown the broken glass, Sarah asked Amanda to give it to her. Then Amanda handed this broken glass to Sarah. Amanda continued to cry and said, *"I don't know what I am doing or where I am going. I just want to die."* Amanda continued and said, *"I am so lonely, I have no friends, no one cares about me. It is better that I am gone."* Sarah said, *"Amanda, please don't harm yourself. Look, I am your friend and Jesus is your best friend. You are not alone anymore. We care about you. This is why we are out here for you."*

Amanda looked Sarah in the eyes and said, *"You are a real nice girl! You have made me feel a little better. I was not supposed to walk through the Town today. But for some reason I was walking down the high street and heard some Christian music, which made me stop and sing along. Then I have met you.*

I am so glad that I have met a good girl like you. You are a real nice person. Sarah will you be my friend forever?" Sarah said, *"Of course I will Amanda, come and see us anytime. While we are apart, please don't forget that Jesus is there with you and cares about you. Don't forget that. He loves you so much. You are worth a million to Jesus. Hold on to Him tightly and He will never let you go. Look yourself in the mirror every day and say I am worth a million to Jesus."* Sarah felt that the Devil was constantly reminding her that she was worth nothing, but after Amanda confessed that she was worth a million to Jesus several times; her face began to look brighter.

Amanda wanted a prayer from Sarah and so they had a time of prayer and thanksgiving. Then Amanda had to leave because of her professional counselling appointment.

We have never seen her since, but we are assured that she repented of her sins and accepted the Lord Jesus as her personal Saviour. We thank the Lord for giving us this opportunity. Jesus saves lives.

Comments from the Public

We had a few people writing us lovely comments and notes to encourage us in our Ministry:

- ➢ "Thank you for your beautiful music and hymns. You have really brightened my day"
- ➢ "Just a note to encourage you...It was so beautiful to hear worship of Jesus in the high street, you blessed my day"
- ➢ "You have lifted up my spirit. You are doing a great work. Your tracts and songs have uplifted me."
- ➢ "You guys are making everyone happy."

Final Call - Back to London

> ➢ "How sweet is the sound you all make. The joy that you share is beyond compare. This Ministry that you have is beautiful and it will increase greatly in the coming weeks. As the Lord wants to take your Ministry around the world."

The Choi Family realised that God had been so faithful to this Ministry in the last ten years. God did not change once and He never failed to give us His love and compassion. The words of the hymn, *'Great is thy faithfulness'* really had come to reality. The words of the hymn also say; ***"Morning by morning new mercies I see; all I have needed thy hand has provided. Great is thy faithfulness, Lord unto me!"*** We feel that we have lived one thousand years and encountered so many experiences, challenges and opportunities in a single day. As a united family, we will continue to serve the Lord until we see God face to face.

Chapter 23

Special Chapter - Funny Moments

Bus Emergency Stop

A lady was so touched by our Singing Ministry; she stood in the middle of the road listening intensively to the music. She did not know the bus was on its way towards her. The bus had to stop and the driver had to get out of the bus and remove her from the road.

Holiday Coach (Company 1)

We thought that the coach holiday was a great way to reach unreachable places such as the North Coast of Cornwall in South West England.

321

This package includes the travel, breakfast and dinner, accommodation and free excursions to local Towns. Therefore, we challenged ourselves to book an eight days package to Newquay. Our suitcase was extremely large because the electronic keyboard had to be inserted in order to share the Gospel. We were a little embarrassed when we handed it over to the driver. He might have warned us that the luggage was too large for this type of a holiday. The driver pulled his face and said, *"Goodness, are you taking a kitchen sink with you? Or is there a dead body in here?"* We laughed, and in fact we had not brought any holiday clothes with us except the necessary equipment to sing in the Town Centre.

Special Chapter - Funny Moments

Holiday Coach (Company 2)

We booked three day package to Somerset and stayed in Wessex hotel. This was a great way to travel down South West of England and to visit local Towns in these areas to share the Gospel. However, when we were heading to our first Town of Glastonbury, the driver reversed the large coach vehicle about nine times. He was the driver and yet he was not sure where he was taking us.

Holiday Coach (Company 3)

We were being used to travelling via the coach holidays. This time we were heading towards the South Coast of England. On Sunday, the excursions were to Plymouth Town Centre. We wanted to head there to sing and share the Gospel. However, according to the driver, the plan was to visit the garden centre first and then to Plymouth Town.

We asked if we could head to Plymouth straight away rather than visit the garden centre. The driver, kindly let all the passengers off at the garden centre and drove us to Plymouth Town Centre. When the driver had picked up the passengers, he said, *"Three folks from South Korea is singing in Plymouth Town Centre, go and watch their performance."* The total of 30 passengers came to us and encouraged us as we were evangelising. When we came back on the coach later that evening, the driver reported positively to the hotel manager and the manager had given us the permission to sing for half an hour. The sharing of the Gospel can be achieved in a various methods. We were so grateful for the driver Philip.

Public Toilet - Portrush, Northern Ireland

One man in the public toilet cubical were whistling hymn and when he came out, he shook David's hand and said the singing and preaching was wonderful.

Special Chapter - Funny Moments

Puppy singing Hymns

David and Hannah were singing and then a little puppy came close to our amplifier and started hauling. The puppy must have thought the music was sad and started to make similar noise. The owner laughed and tried to pull the puppy away from the amplifier but the puppy refused to go home.

Complaint Letter - Lisburn, Northern Ireland

A lady from the newspaper agency had come out to stop us from evangelising. Our luggage suitcase handle was next to us. She slotted the letter inside the handle. The wind that day was severe, so Sarah pulled out the letter and let it go, flying in the wind. This lady had to run after it and grabbed hold of her complaint letter and rushed back into her office with a red face, feeling embarrassed.

Chapter 24

Additional Notes

This chapter includes a list of people who came to know the Lord Jesus Christ through our singing ministry; and a list of people who have been healed from their diseases.

Turning back to Jesus

➢ Caroline gave her life to Jesus - Coventry, England

➢ Agi repented of her sins and gave her life to Jesus - Walsall, England

➢ Denise was religious Catholic, wanting to have full relationship with Jesus - Western Supermare, England

- ➢ Terry who had backslidden had recommitted his life to Christ - Stockton on Tees, England

- ➢ Malcolm who was a drug addict, committed his life to Jesus in Stockton-on-Tees, England

- ➢ One alcoholic and homeless gave his life to Jesus - Limerick, Ireland

- ➢ One drunken man rebuked the Gospel for three days and on the fourth day, he confessed to follow Jesus. - Galway, Ireland

- ➢ One alcoholic - who had caused a lot of trouble by stealing from and abusing the Choi Family for a couple of years, came to us one day and repented of his sins, he apologised for his behaviour, paid back double what he had stolen from us and he committed his life to Christ Jesus - Coleraine, Northern Ireland

- ➢ An Italian guy heard the Gospel for half an hour and made a new commitment to follow Jesus - Neath, England

- ➢

Additional Notes

- Mrs Joan Daglish heard the Gospel, then cried with repentance and now has made a commitment to follow Jesus. - North Shield, England
- Amanda wanted to end her life, then heard the music, cried with repentance and confessed "*I want Jesus in my life*" - Sutton London, England
- 60 people gave their lives to Christ - Lisburn, Northern Ireland
- 300 people gave their lives to Christ - Coleraine, Northern Ireland

Healed from Sicknesses

- A lady with fits were healed from her disease after prayer (Nursing home) -Halesowen, England
- Sophie- who had stomach pain over 20 years had been healed in Coleraine, Northern Ireland

- Margaret - who had black toes and swollen feet for many years were healed from sickness in Antrim, Northern Ireland
- Jack - whole of his life, he had trouble sleeping and had been healed after prayer in Antrim, Northern Ireland
- Paul - who had migraines for six months. Doctors medication could not help him but after a prayer he had been healed - England
- Jack - who had cataracts in his eyes were healed - England
- Navel- healed from depression and issues relating to his brain - Coleraine, Northern Ireland
- John - swollen face healed after prayer - Stockton on Tees, England
- Lily - cataracts in one eye, finding it difficult to see, healed after prayer - Coleraine, Northern Ireland
- Betty - red sores near chest, healed after prayer - Coleraine, Northern Ireland

Postscript

I hope you have been challenged, encouraged and inspired by reading this book. These mission trips have been exciting, and at times, risky and dangerous. Even to the occasions when we had barking dogs set upon us! However, the Lord had been with us during these journeys, helping us in the times of trouble. The Lord used three ordinary people, who had been brought up in a poor community, extremely fragile and weak, who had no educational background to do the work of the Lord. The Lord had transformed our family from nothing to something. When our family was into circular world and did not fully obey the will of God, we were hopeless, and had no unity in the family. After repenting of our sins and walking close to Jesus daily, the Lord brought unity in the family and showed us many miracles in our lives. Let me finish this book by quoting you a verse from the Gospel song, *"I don't know about tomorrow."* These words speak about our future: ***I don't know about tomorrow, I just live from day to day. I don't worry over the future for I know what Jesus said. And today I will walk beside Him for He knows what is ahead. Many things about tomorrow I don't seem to understand but I know who holds tomorrow and I know who holds my hand.***

Indeed, Jesus knows our future and when we walk beside him, He will take care of our lives. During the time I wrote this book, there had been five consecutive terrorist attacks in the UK in the space of three months. Westminster attack (22nd March), suicide bombing attack in Manchester (22nd May), London Bridge attack (3rd June), deadly fire attack at Grenfell Tower (14th June) and Finsbury Park attack (19th June). We can never predict our tomorrow and therefore we must come back to Jesus. One thing we are certain of is that if you trust in the Lord as your own personal Saviour, you will spend Eternity with Him (Jesus) in Heaven.

"Most assuredly, I say to you he who believes in me (Jesus) has everlasting life." John 6:47 (NKJV)